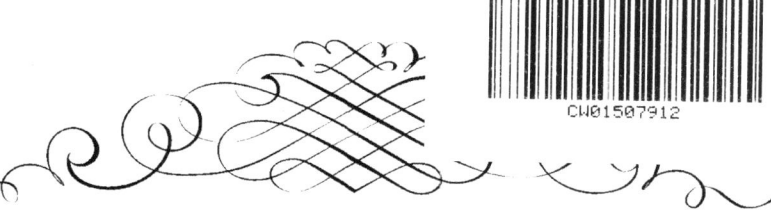
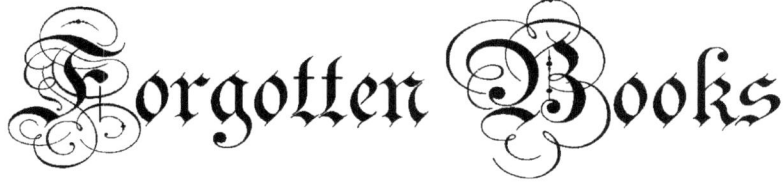
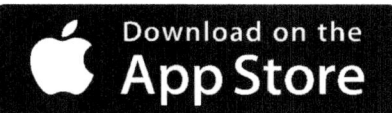
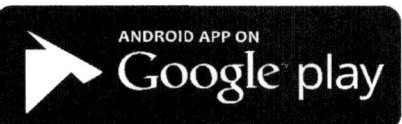

ISBN 978-1-330-11255-7
PIBN 10028723

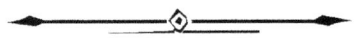

English
Français
Deutsche
Italiano
Español
Português

www.forgottenbooks.com

Mythology Photography **Fiction**
Fishing Christianity **Art** Cooking
Essays Buddhism Freemasonry
Medicine **Biology** Music **Ancient**
Egypt Evolution Carpentry Physics
Dance Geology **Mathematics** Fitness
Shakespeare **Folklore** Yoga Marketing
Confidence Immortality Biographies
Poetry **Psychology** Witchcraft
Electronics Chemistry History **Law**
Accounting **Philosophy** Anthropology
Alchemy Drama Quantum Mechanics
Atheism Sexual Health **Ancient History**
Entrepreneurship Languages Sport
Paleontology Needlework Islam
Metaphysics Investment Archaeology
Parenting Statistics Criminology
Motivational

CATALOGUE OF PAINTINGS
BY JOAQUÍN SOROLLA Y BASTIDA

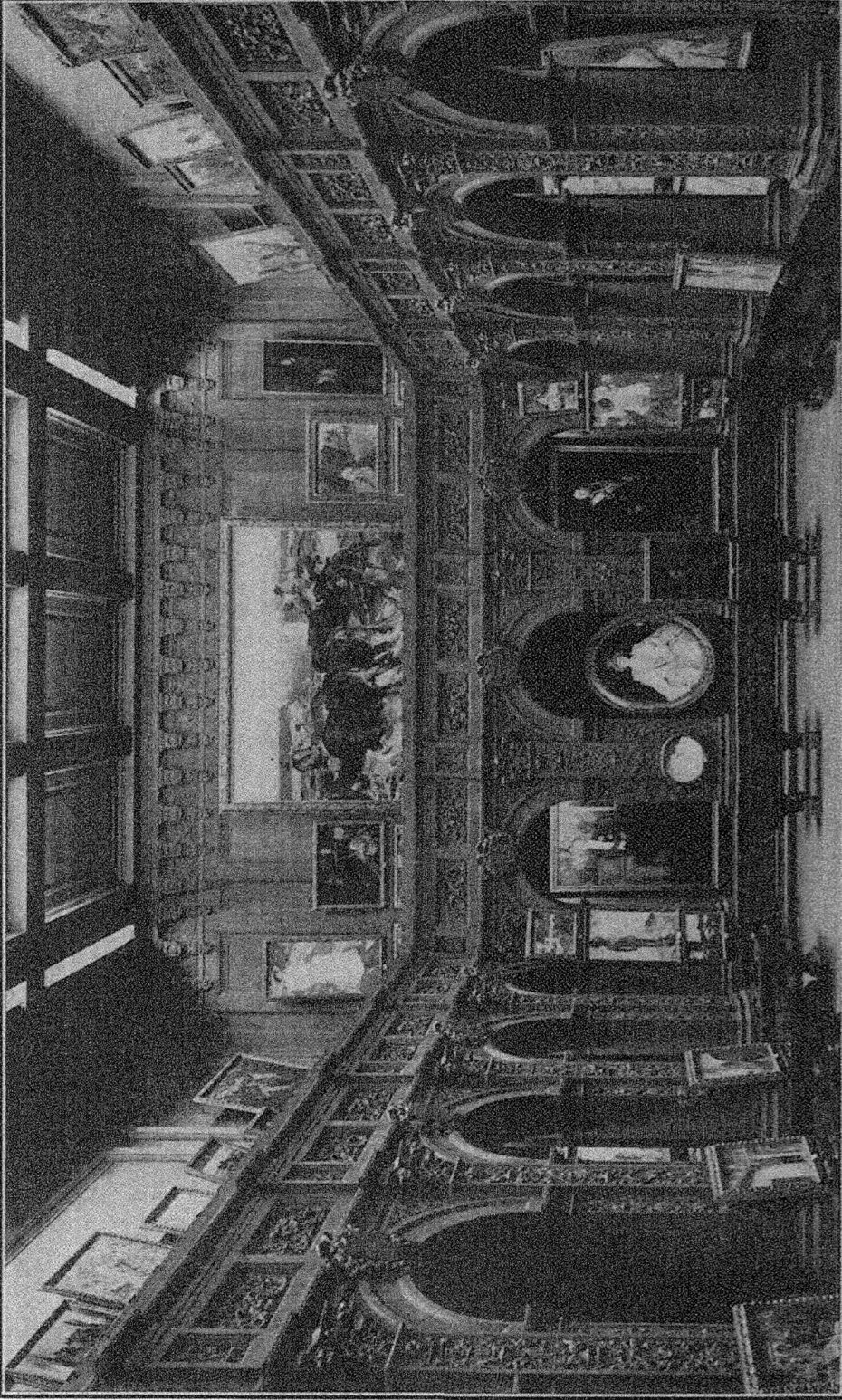

CATALOGUE OF PAINTINGS
BY JOAQUÍN SOROLLA Y BASTIDA

EXHIBITED BY

THE HISPANIC SOCIETY OF AMERICA

FEBRUARY 8 TO MARCH 8, 1909

WITH INTRODUCTION BY
LEONARD WILLIAMS

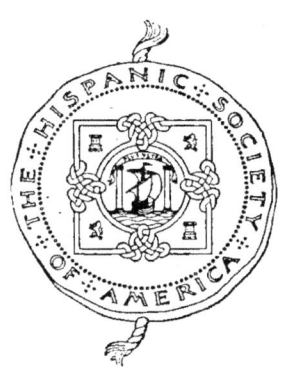

THE HISPANIC SOCIETY OF AMERICA
NEW YORK 1909

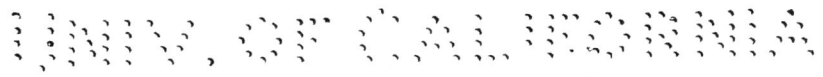

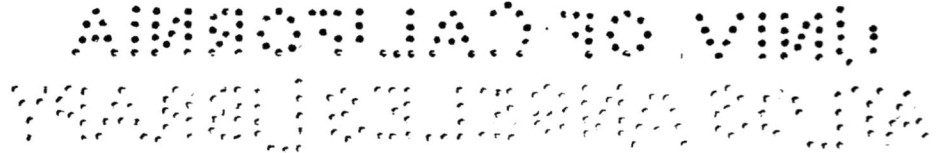

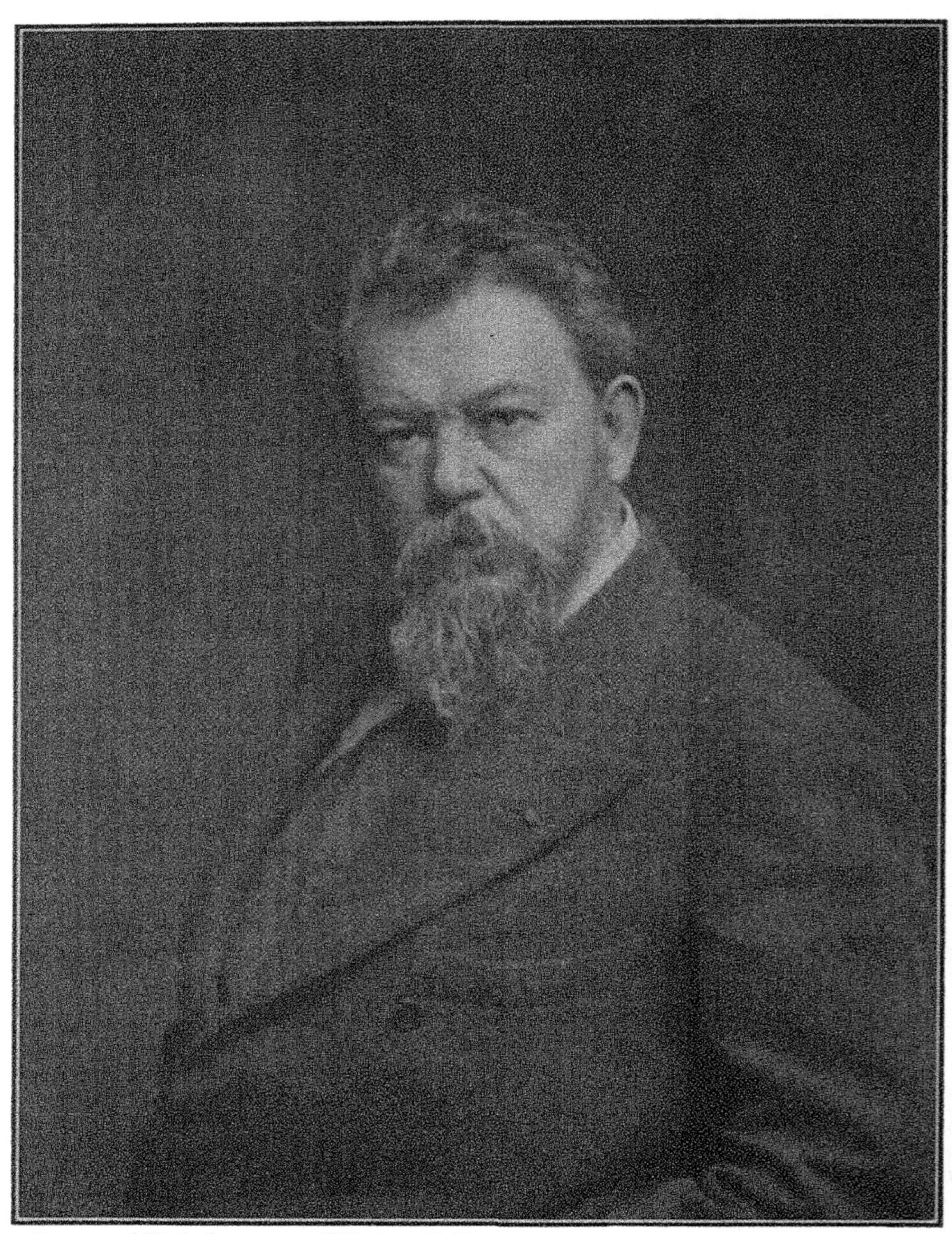

Courtesy of W. A. Cooper, 297 Fifth Ave., N. Y.

THE ART OF
JOAQUÍN SOROLLA

BY

LEONARD WILLIAMS

THE ART OF
JOAQUÍN SOROLLA

I

BIOGRAPHICAL

JOAQUÍN SOROLLA, the son of humble parents, was born at Valencia, Spain, on February 27, 1863. Two years later, the cholera epidemic which was raging in that city carried off both his father and his mother, and the orphan, together with his infant sister, was adopted by his aunt upon the mother's side, Doña Isabel Bastida, and her husband, Don José Piqueres.

When Joaquin was of an age to go to school, he manifested little inclination for his studies proper, though he revealed a stealthy and incorrigible craze for scrawling embryonic drawings in his copy-books, until, impressed by the precocious merit and persistence of this extra-pedagogic labor, one of his masters was intelligent enough to overlook his inattention to the tasks appointed him, and even made him surreptitious presents of material for the prosecution of his hobby.

In course of time, since young Sorolla made no visible progress at his lessons, his uncle, who was by trade a locksmith, removed the boy from school and placed him in his workshop, while yet allowing him to attend some drawing-classes, held at a local school for artisans; and here his resolution and his talent swept off all the prizes; so that, on reaching fifteen years, he was permitted to renounce the locksmith's shop and finally devote himself to studying art.

He now became a student of the Academia de Bellas Artes of San Carlos, which is also at Valencia, and won, almost immediately, the triple prize for coloring, drawing from the model, and perspective. About this time, too, he received assistance from a philanthropic gentleman named Garcia (whose daughter, Doña Clotilde, he subsequently married), and so was able to remain for several years at the academy. During these years he visited Madrid on three occasions, and exhibited, first of all, three paintings which aroused no curiosity, and afterward his earliest important work, namely, a canvas of large dimensions titled "The Second of May." The second visit to the Spanish capital was longer than the other two, and young Sorolla utilized it to his best advantage by copying the masterpieces of Velazquez and Ribera in the Prado Gallery.

"The Second of May,"[1] which represents the desperate resistance of the *Madrileños* to the French invading army, during the Spanish War of Independence, is by no means a flawless work, although the drawing is correct and spirited; nor is it even an unusually precocious effort for a painter who was more than twenty years of age. Yet it contained one striking innovation; for it was painted in the open air, Sorolla choosing for his natural and informal studio the arena of the spacious bull-ring of Valencia, where he enwreathed his models with dense smoke in scrupulous reconstitution of authentic scenes of war.

In the same year (1884), another of his paintings won for him the scholarship offered by his native town for studying art in Italy. Accordingly, he repaired to Rome and stayed there for some months, proceeding thence to Paris, and returning not long afterward to the Italian capital. However, at the exhibitions, held in Paris, of the works of Bastien-Lepage and Menzel, "Sorolla's eyes were opened to

[1] This painting is now in the Biblioteca-Museo Balaguer, founded with the expenditure of almost his whole fortune by the eminent Catalan poet, historian, and statesman, Victor Balaguer, at Villanueva y Geltrú, a town in Cataluña.

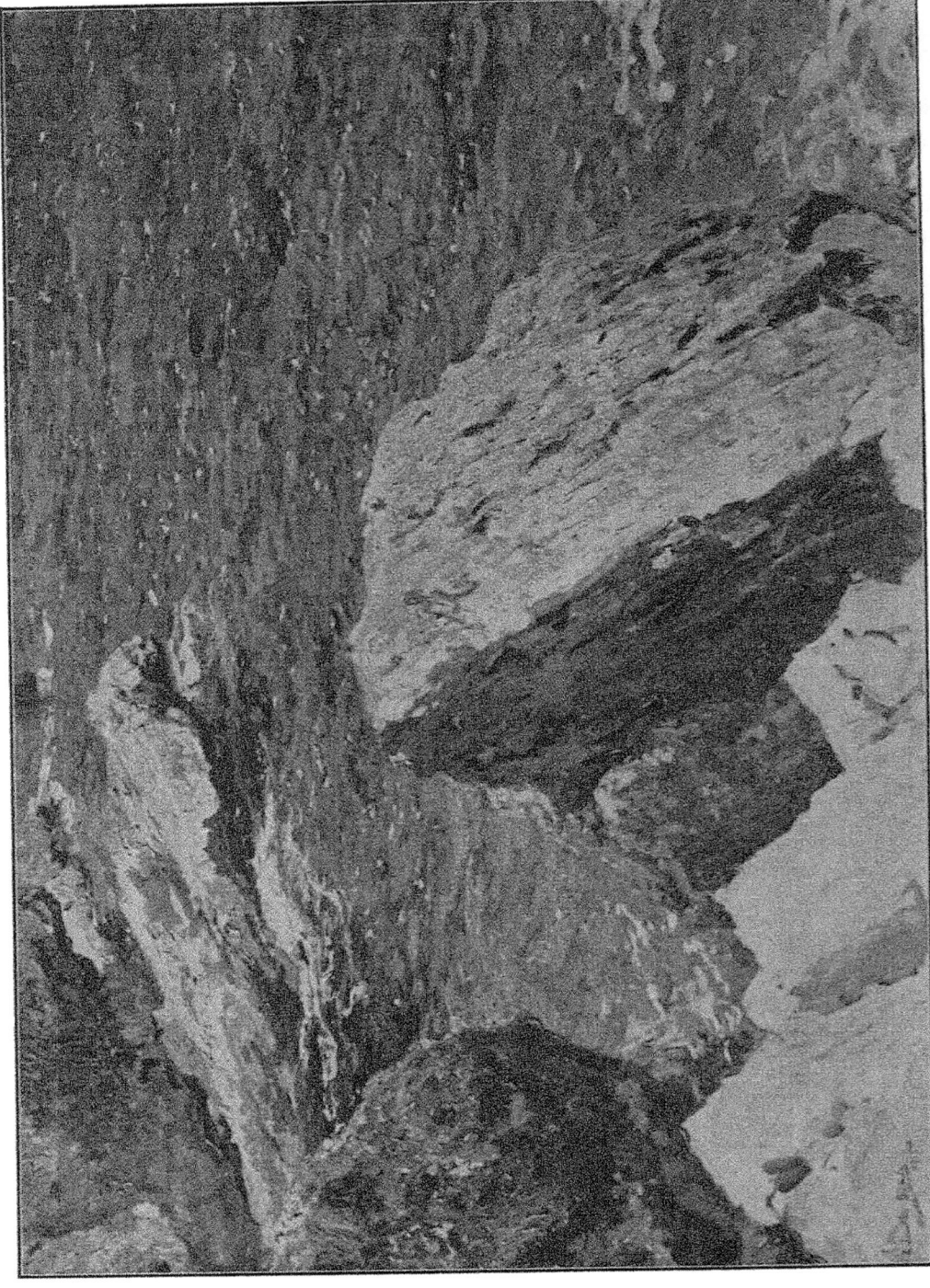

the revolution which was being effected in the history of modern painting";[1] and even after his return to Italy, this novel and regenerative movement in French art continued to engage his preference. Already, therefore, in the opening stage of his career, the youthful and spontaneous realist of Valencia— the compatriot of Goya and the fellow-citizen of Spagnoletto—was captivated and encouraged by the parallel yet independent realism of a German and a French contemporary.

On his return to Rome, where false and academic methods still pretended to their old supremacy, Sorolla, led by duty rather than by desire, produced a large religious painting titled "The Burial of the Saviour," marked by his wonted excellence of color and of line, but not appreciably inspired by any sentiment of deep devotion. This work, upon its exhibition at Madrid in 1887, attracted some attention, but was not rewarded with a medal. Two other paintings, also shown about this time, disclose the true direction of Sorolla's sympathy. The one, titled "Un Boulevard de Paris," somewhat impressionistic in the manner of Pissaro, depicts a busy evening scene outside a large café. The other subject is a

[1] "Joaquin Sorolla y Bastida," by Aureliano de Beruete, published in "La Lectura," January, 1901.

sketch of a Parisian girl, treated in the simple, realistic style of Bastien-Lepage, and therefore quite emancipated from the harsh eclecticism of the Roman school.

While visiting Italy for the second time, Sorolla made a longish sojourn at Assisi, copying the old Italian masters, as well as doing original work subtly yet happily associated with the peasant-author of the "Saison d'Octobre." During the next three years he painted, among a number of other works, "A Procession at Burgos in the Sixteenth Century," "After the Bath" (a life-sized female figure standing nude against a background of white marble), and the well-known "Otra Margarita" ("Another Marguerite"). This latter, now at St. Louis in America, represents a girl belonging to the humblest class, who has been guilty of infanticide, and whom the Civil Guard convey as prisoner to receive or to perform her sentence. The scene is a third-class railway-wagon, bare, uncushioned, comfortless—such as is still not obsolete in Spain. The head of this unhappy "Marguerite" is drooping on her breast and, with her blanched, emaciated face and limp, dejected form, denotes the utmost depth of human woe. Her hands are bound, but a fold of her coarse shawl has partly fallen or been drawn across them. A bundle lies beside her on

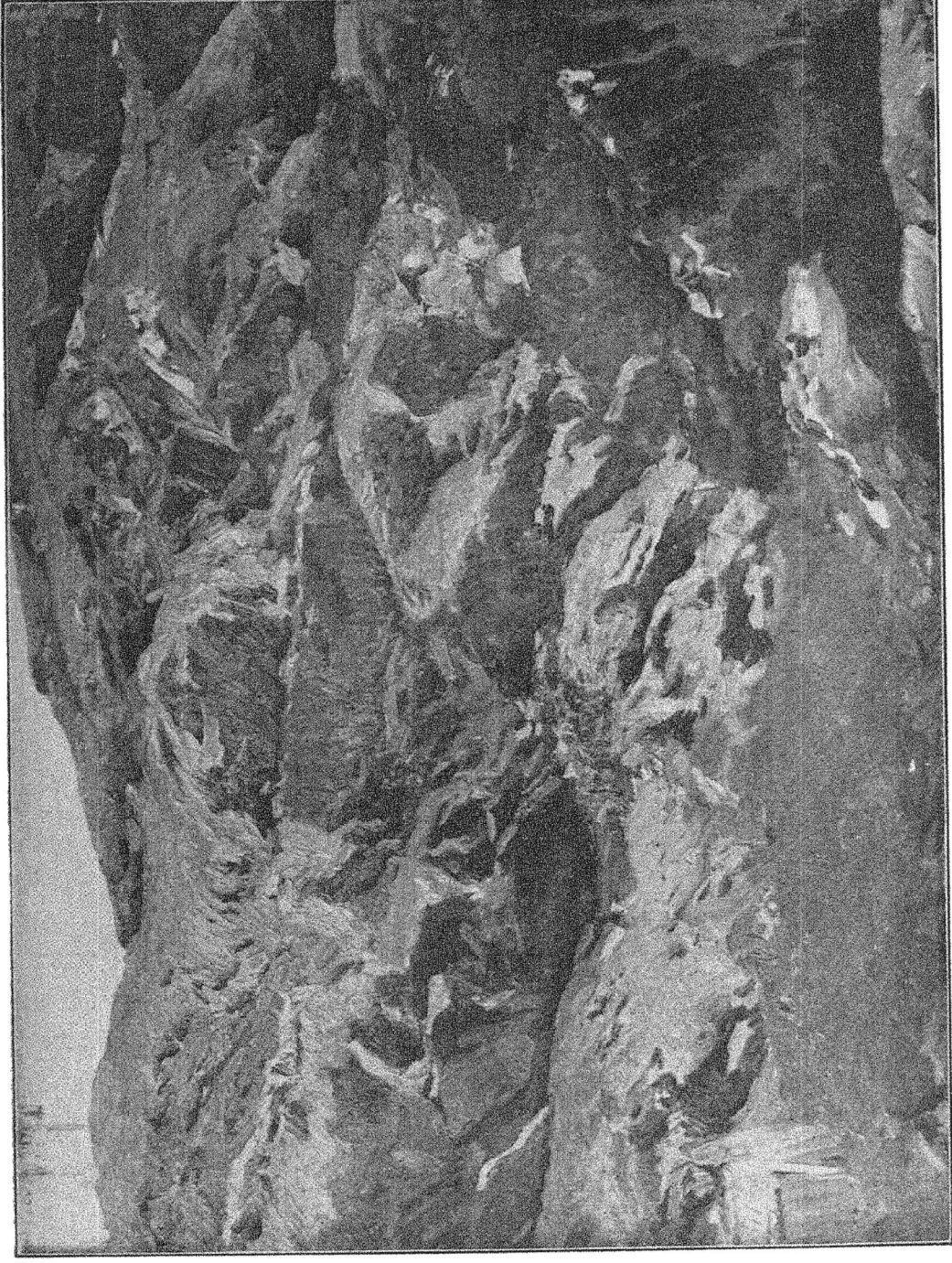

the seat. Though it is painted out with care, this work has scarcely any scope for detail. Nothing relieves its melancholy bareness save the spots upon the prisoner's cheap print dress, and the pattern on the kerchief which contains her change of clothing.

This pitiful and somber scene is treated with a poignant realism, yet with an equally eloquent restraint. Emotion here is not obtruded, as in the case of mediocre genre: it is not ostentatious, but suggestive. Flawless in technical fidelity, the figure of the girl discloses that her moral weariness has overcome her physical. Her attitude of collapse proceeds, not from a muscular fatigue, as much as from an agony of remorse which has its fountain in her very soul. One of her two custodians marks her with a meditative and compassionate eye, puzzled, it may be, at the vagaries of the law devised by man, and speculating why its undivided wrath must here be visited upon the frail accomplice.

Other important paintings executed by Sorolla at this time are named "The Happy Day," "Kissing the Relic," and "Blessing the Fishing-Boat." The subjects of the latter two are indicated by their titles. A beautiful and touching moment is recorded in "The Happy Day." A little fisher-girl, who has received her first Communion on this "happy morn" kisses,

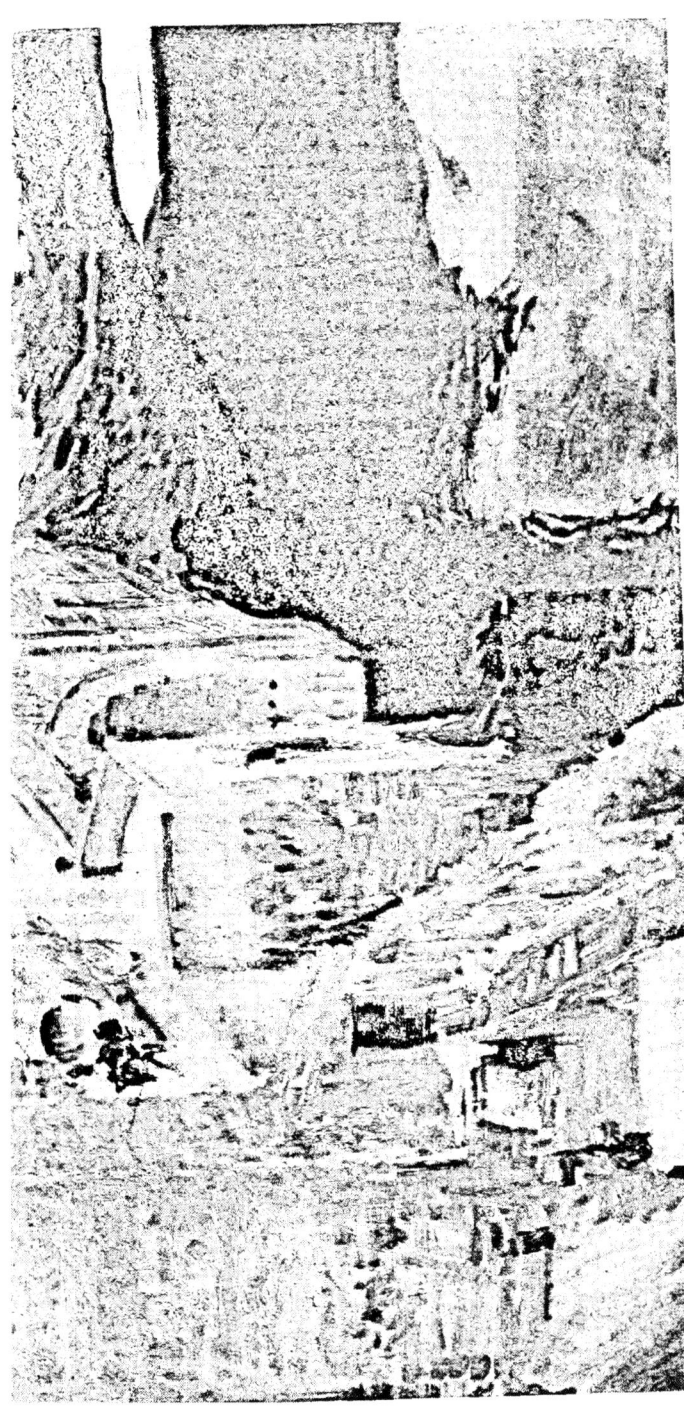

on reaching home, the hand of her blind grand-father. The cottage-door is open, and the sunlight, streaming through, lavishes its pure caresses on the gossamer clouds of her communion-veil.

In this or the succeeding year, two of Sorolla's paintings were exhibited at the Salon. Their titles are, "The White-Slave Traffic" and "The Fishing-Boat's Return."[1] The former is at present in Amer ica; the latter (which had been classified "Hors Con-cours") was purchased for the Luxembourg.

The subjects of these two great paintings offer an extraordinary contrast. The figures in the first are weary women, huddled together, dozing and lethar-gic, in a narrow, low-toned, somber railway carriage. But in the other work, the busy characters that plash and plunge about the water's edge respire a very sur-feit of vitality; fishers and cattle bringing in the boat, enlivened and illuminated by the glorious sun-shine of Valencia.

Between that period and the present day, we are confronted, in Sorolla's art, with marvelous, well-nigh miraculous fecundity and quality, interpreting all aspects and developments of contemporary Spain portraits of royal personages, nobles, commoners,

[1] Sorolla's "Beaching the Boat" (318) repeats the same majes-tic motive on a larger scale.

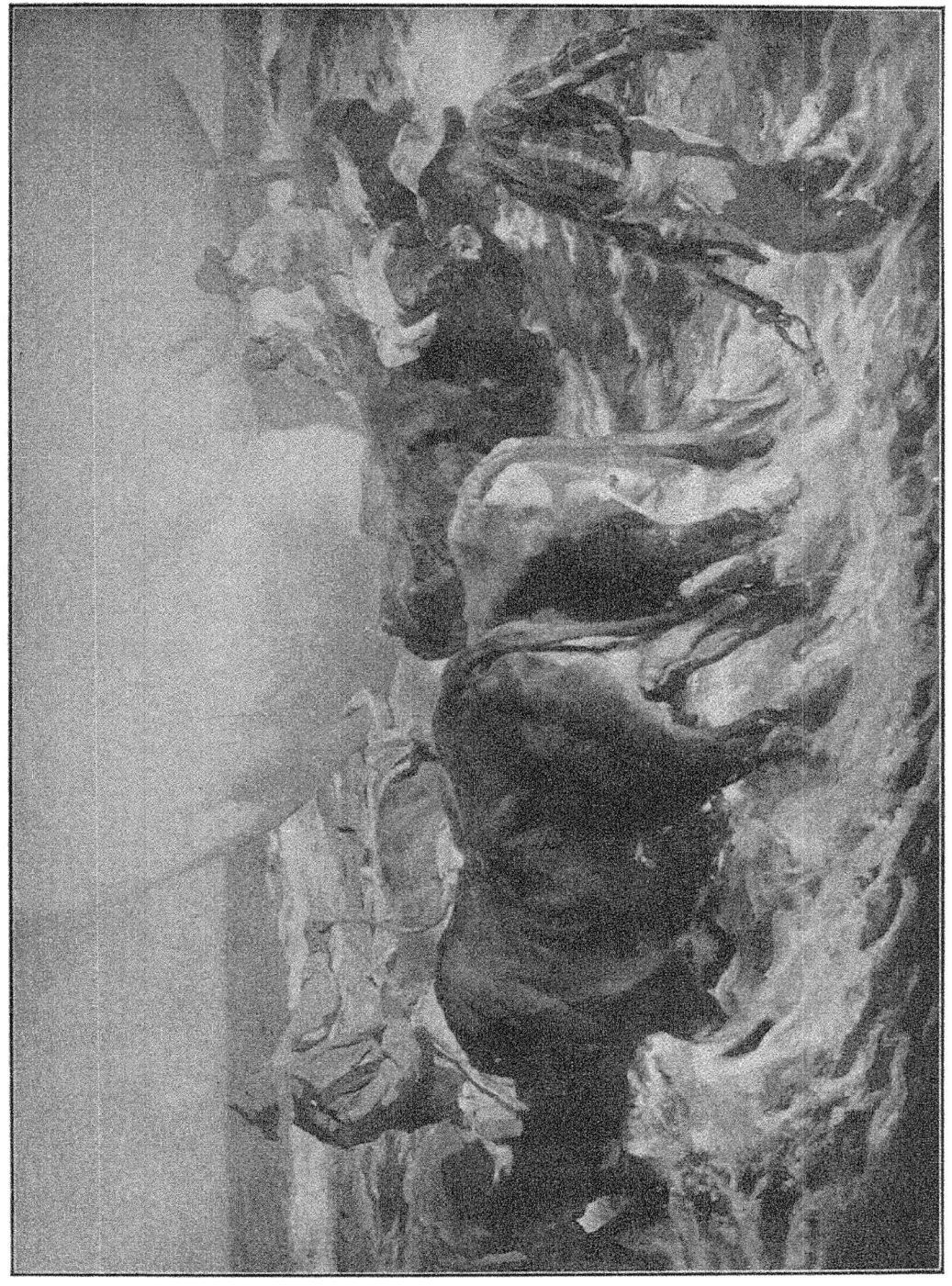

of the artist's wife and children, of statesmen, novel-
ists, poets, scientists, or soldiers; landscape and prospects of the naked sea; the bright and tender joys
of infant life, the playful scenes of boyhood and of
girlhood, sorrows and problems and anxieties of
later age, the sordid schemes of evil-doers, the stren-
uous toilers of the deep, the simple cultivators of the
soil, the village cares and pastimes of the peasantry.

Such paintings are (to quote the titles of a very
few), "Sewing the Sail,"[1] "The Beach of Valencia,"
"A Scientific Experiment," "The Raisin-Dressers,"
"The Wounded Fisherman," "A Sad Inheritance,"
and "The Bath."

This latter represents the seaside at Valencia,
"whose manifold charms this artist renders so felici-
tously. A woman with her back to us unfolds a
sheet, in which she is about to wrap a baby whom
another woman holds. The little one is naked, and
his limbs are stiffened by the cold sensation of his
bath. Behind them is the sea, furrowed by fishing-
boats with swollen sails, illuminated by the golden
glory of a Spanish summer's morning."[2]

This jocund theme presents a striking contrast

---

[1] Shown at Madrid, the Salon, Munich (Gold Medal), Vienna
(Gold Medal), and the Paris Exhibition, where the artist was
awarded the Grand Prix for his "Triste Herencia." "Sewing
the Sail" is now the property of the Venice Corporation.

[2] Beruete, *op. cit.*

with "A Sad Inheritance."[1]   Here also is the fore-
shore of Valencia, though it is specked and vivified
no longer by those dancing sails and animated figures.
An air of sudden and depressing gloom seems to have
overcrept the water and the sunshine.   Even so quick
are nature's moods to echo back our own.   For here
are not the vigorous fisher-folk, able to work and
strive, able to win their independent bread.   Instead
of such, we contemplate a score or so of imbecile or
crippled boys, the inmates of a house of refuge for
the cast-off children of depraved and unknown parents.   The stern, robust, and noble figure of a priest,
towering above this orphaned and pathetic gathering
of frail humanity, extends a shielding arm over some
two or three.   Weighed down by helplessness and
shame, these joyless creatures are not scurrying
through the sand, or blithely plashing in the breakers.
The gaiety of healthy boyhood is denied to them.
Their drooping attitudes are inert, morose, and
plaintive, while, as it were infected by the agony and
pity of it all, the color of the sea is leaden, and the
sun throws out no cheerful and invigorating ra-
diance, but is merely sultry.

[1] This picture hangs in the Sunday-school room of the
Church of the Ascension, Fifth Avenue and Tenth Street, New
York City.   It is kindly lent to the Hispanic Society of
America as illustrating a distinct type of mastery, by the cour-
tesy of its owner, John E. Berwind, Esq., and of the Rector,
the Rev. Percy Stickney Grant.

II

CRITICAL

THE march of art in modern Spain has coincided with her evolution generally. When, in the eighteenth century, the French or Bourbon kings were settled on the throne of Spain, the very life-breath of this nation emanated from Versailles; so that, in order to respire at all, the luckless Spaniards were compelled to simulate a sympathy with, and ape the manners of, a race whose character is radically different from their own. Even their literature declined into a tawdry imitation of the French, replacing natural and sparkling gems by dull and worthless paste; the typical, vital, and inimitable picaresque by nerveless and ephemeral travesties of Gallic forms and Gallic modes of feeling. Nor did the Spanish painters seek a less humiliating destiny. Born in a shallow, pleasure-loving, empty-headed, empty-hearted age, themselves devoid of natural ability, unstimulated by the spur of popular approval. of veracious and ennobling art, they made no effort

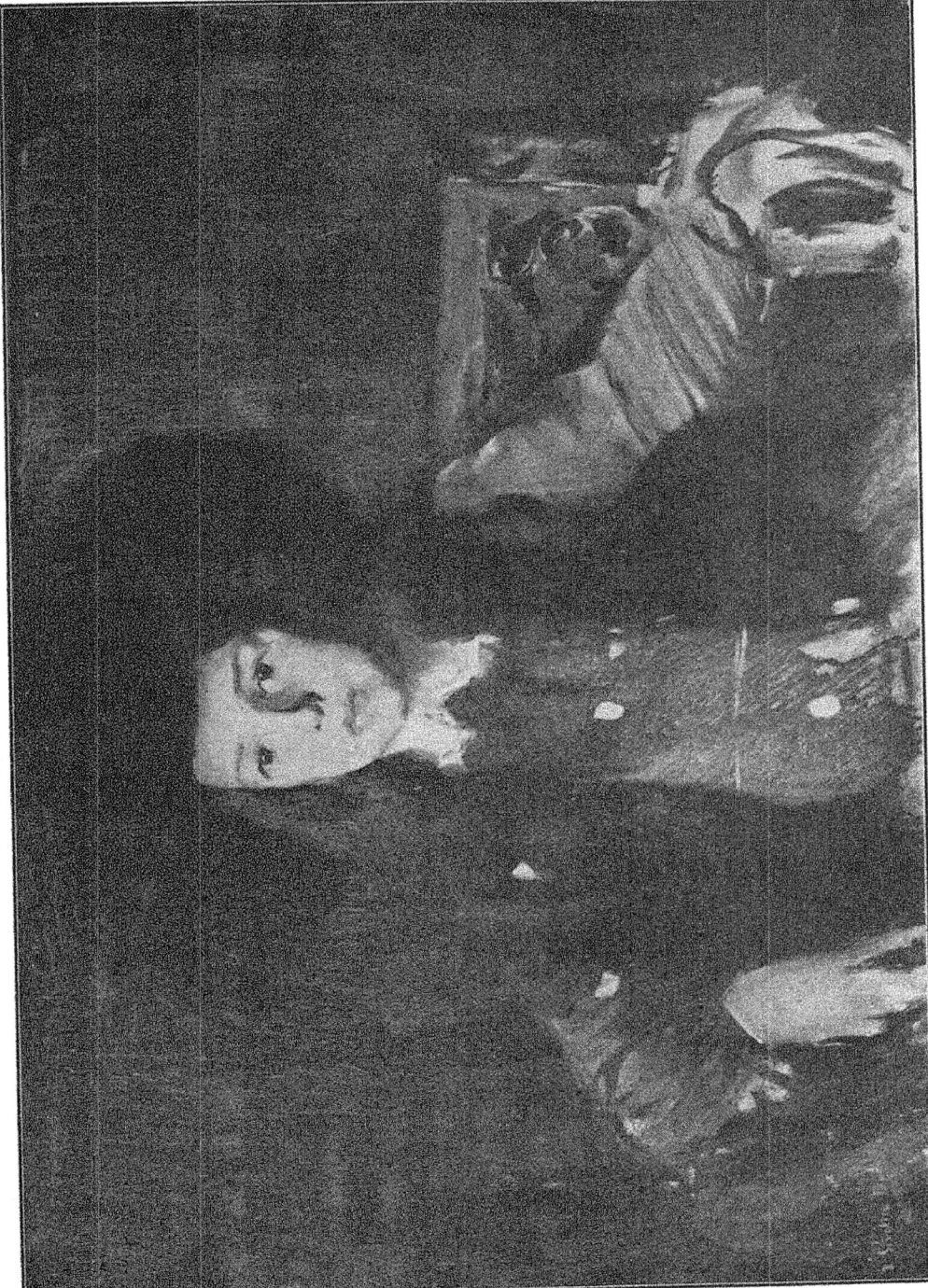

to shake off the cold, unedifying tutelage of Amiconi, Giaquinto, Mengs, and other leaders of the stilted academic school which in those days was tyrannizing over Europe.

Such, of the so-called painters of that lamentable and degenerate time, were Ferro, and Gonzalez Velazquez, Bayeu, Castillo, and Maella—names that have nearly perished with the mediocrities who bore them. Excepting one alone, the rest of Spanish artists were no better. For in this sterile wilderness of weeds, one flower sprang up unchoked and reached its plenitude of beauty and maturity; one bright though solitary beacon cast its cheering glow across these gloomy decades of frivolity, corruption, and routine.

Francisco Goya is the second in importance of all Spanish painters. His life and work alike require to be summed up in contradictory and complex terms. Sprung from the humblest class, the son of simple tillers of the soil,[1] he grew to be a courtier and the pampered confidant of princes; and yet he never weeded out the primitive rudeness from his peasant temper. A coarse, uneducated man, his character, though greatly resolute in certain crises, was swayed

[1] Goya was born on March 30 or 31, 1746, at Fuendetodos, a wretched village in a sparsely populated part of Aragon.

[24]

alternately by generous and by ignoble feeling. His sense of humor was inherently profound; but it obtained together with a rooted disbelief in human good, so that a mingled and discordant bitterness attends his very laughter. This taint of pessimism caused him to bestow his preferential notice on the uglier side of life—its elements of cowardice or fanaticism, of avarice, hypocrisy, or sensuality—and hence his characters, though admirably truthful in the main, seldom excite our pleasurable interest. Although at heart a democrat and revolutionary, and an unaffected hater of oppression and oppressive institutions, such as the army, church, and aristocracy of Spain while these were influenced by the earlier Bourbons, he was, notwithstanding, from time to time, himself a sycophant or tyrant. His sturdy self-reliance frequently assumed the form of arrant and offensive selfishness. His intimacy with the elevated classes wrought him chiefly harm. Viewing their vices with a thinly veiled contempt, he lacked the moral stamina to guard himself from their good-nature and complete his life-work unsupported by their patronage. His correspondence, written in a tumid, egotistic style, confirms his greed of money and of fame; which greed, although his art is Spanish to the core, seduced his private conduct from the patriotic path, and caused him to accept, with unbecoming haste, a salaried yet opprobrious commission from the French usurper.[1]

His work embraces every class of subject—portraiture and genre, pure landscape, mistitled renderings of biblical history,[2] popular and rustic scenes, with or without a landscape setting, studies and sketches in the *picaresco* mood, uniting sarcasm with drollery. We note in him, as Pedro de Madrazo has declared, "the realism of Velazquez, the fantasy of Hogarth, the energy of Rembrandt, the delicacy of Titian, Veronese, and Watteau." Powerless to create imaginative pictures of the future or the past, he viewed the life about him with an actual, robust regard, focusing his undistracted vision on the present only. His art, while yet conspicuously original, reveals throughout the influence of Velazquez; for though he did not imitate that mighty realist, he learned from him to look at nature with a clear, direct, truth-seeking eye. His love of brilliant colors, finely juxtaposed or blended with consummate taste, seems to have been suggested by Tiepolo; for while

[1] Namely, to choose, in company with the painters Napoli and Maella, the representative collection of old masters which was removed to Paris by Napoleon.

[2] I say mistitled, for all of Goya's so-called mythological or sacred characters are faithful portraits of the people of his time.

the coloring of Velazquez is restrained and sad, Goya's is the very soul of brilliancy. The sitters of Velazquez wear a look of indolence and boredom· Goya's are pulsing with the very *joie de la vie*. His rendering of popular and rustic life has all the honest spontaneity of Teniers. His figures, even when roughly and precipitately drawn, possess immense vitality. His kings and queens, his courtiers and his peasants—all have "business and desire." They move, and breathe, and speak to us. They are our intimates, and manifest their moment and this painter's in the restless and romantic history of Spain; just as the figures of Velazquez manifest their co-existence with the ceremonious Hapsburg dynasty of melancholy, semi-moribund Castile.

Both Goya and Velazquez are supremely representative of Spanish painting in a comprehensive sense, as well as of the social character of Spain precisely as it coincided with their several lives and life-work. Each of these two great masters has immortalized the Spanish century which was his own, and further, each was constitutionally suited to his native century. For the high-born painter of the two was the child of an aristocratic age, and the low-born painter was the child of a plebeian—or (if I may coin the word) plebeianized age. This happy fact has caused them to bequeath to us the absolute historic truth; for Spain beneath the Hapsburg rule was eminently jealous and observant of her Visigothic and blue-blooded origin, and Spain beneath the rule of the Bourbons was eminently *parvenu* and vulgar. It has been truthfully remarked that something of the aristocrat breathes in the lowliest sitters of Velazquez. Conversely, something of the ignobly born breathes in the most exalted sitters of Goya.

In these consecutive yet eminently different periods in the history of the Peninsula, we note a century of native and ancestral haughtiness and *hidalguía,* followed by a century of enervating foppery introduced from France. During the centuries of Hapsburg rule, it was regarded as a deep disgrace for even the humble classes to pursue a trade, and nearly all the trades in the Peninsula were exercised by foreigners, who consumed her energies just as the foreigner is consuming British energies to-day

Goya died and was buried at Bordeaux in 1828. He left no pupils worthy to be thus denominated; so that his influence, though destined to develop more and more as time rolled on, has only operated at a lengthy distance from his death. The cause of this was simple. Spain, in the opening quarter of the nineteenth century, was too distracted by internal

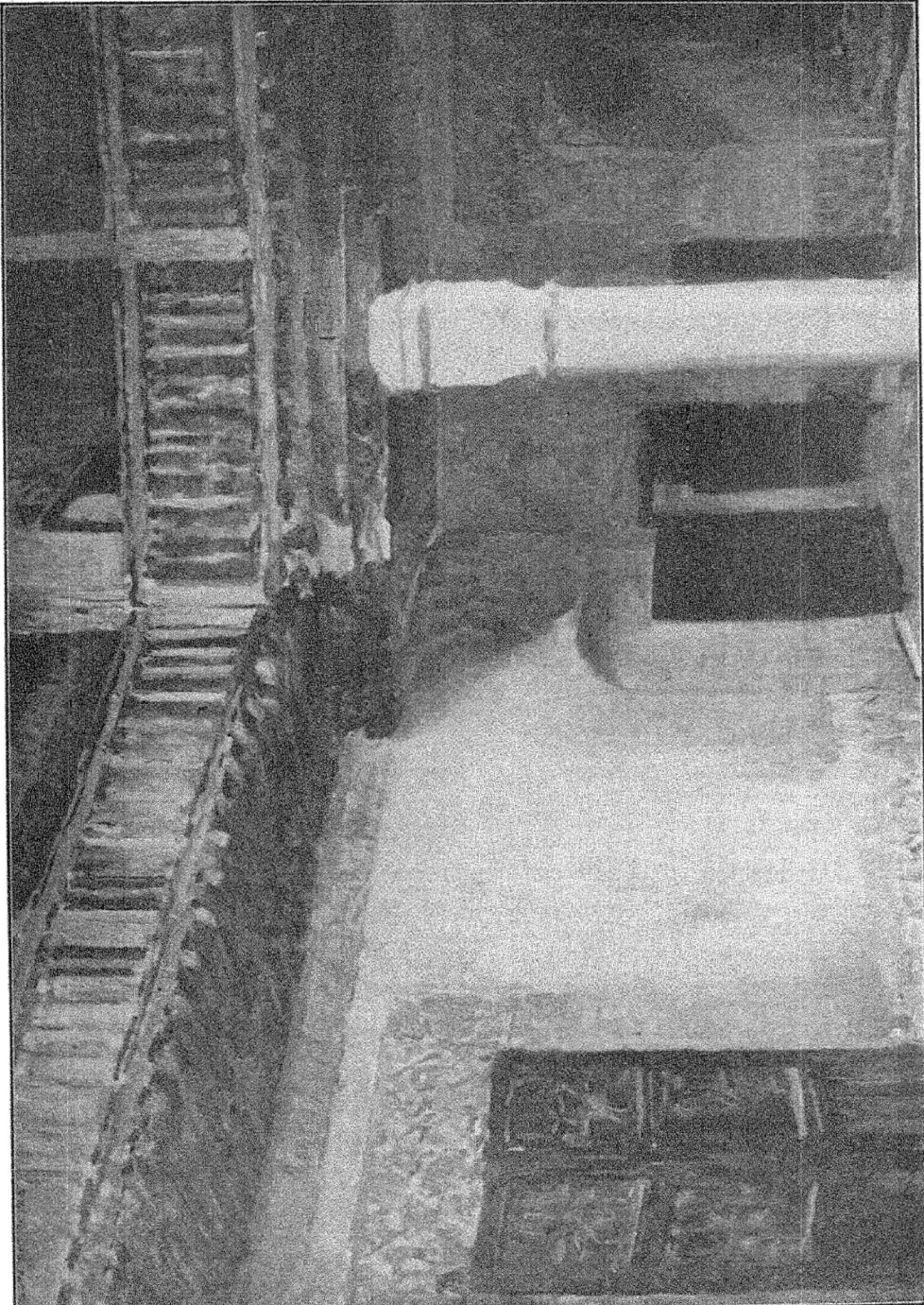

strife, as well as by the foreigner's tempestuous invasion of her soil, to turn her troubled eyes to art. When she recovered from the nightmare grasp of those calamities, she found herself the child of other times and other tendencies. A second period of French influence—that of David and his pompous sect—had now succeeded to the cold academism of the previous century. This newer influence, conveyed across the Pyrenees by Juan Ribera, José Aparicio, and José de Madrazo—three Spanish painters whose inborn ability was spoiled by their Parisian training—was but a borrowed and reflected light at best, and rapidly flickered out in Spain, just as the parent light had flickered out in France.

The romantic movement crossed the Spanish frontier toward the year 1835; yet its effect was unregenerative here, because, as I have shown, it sprang from a factitious and delusive origin. Among the ardent and impressionable sons of Spain who gave their unconditional allegiance to this movement, were three unquestionably gifted poets—Zorrilla, Espronceda, and the Duke of Rivas; but since the talent and enthusiasm of her painters were by no means so pronounced, it acted on these latter far less powerfully. It has even been said that art in the Peninsula remained entirely unaffected by the French Roman-

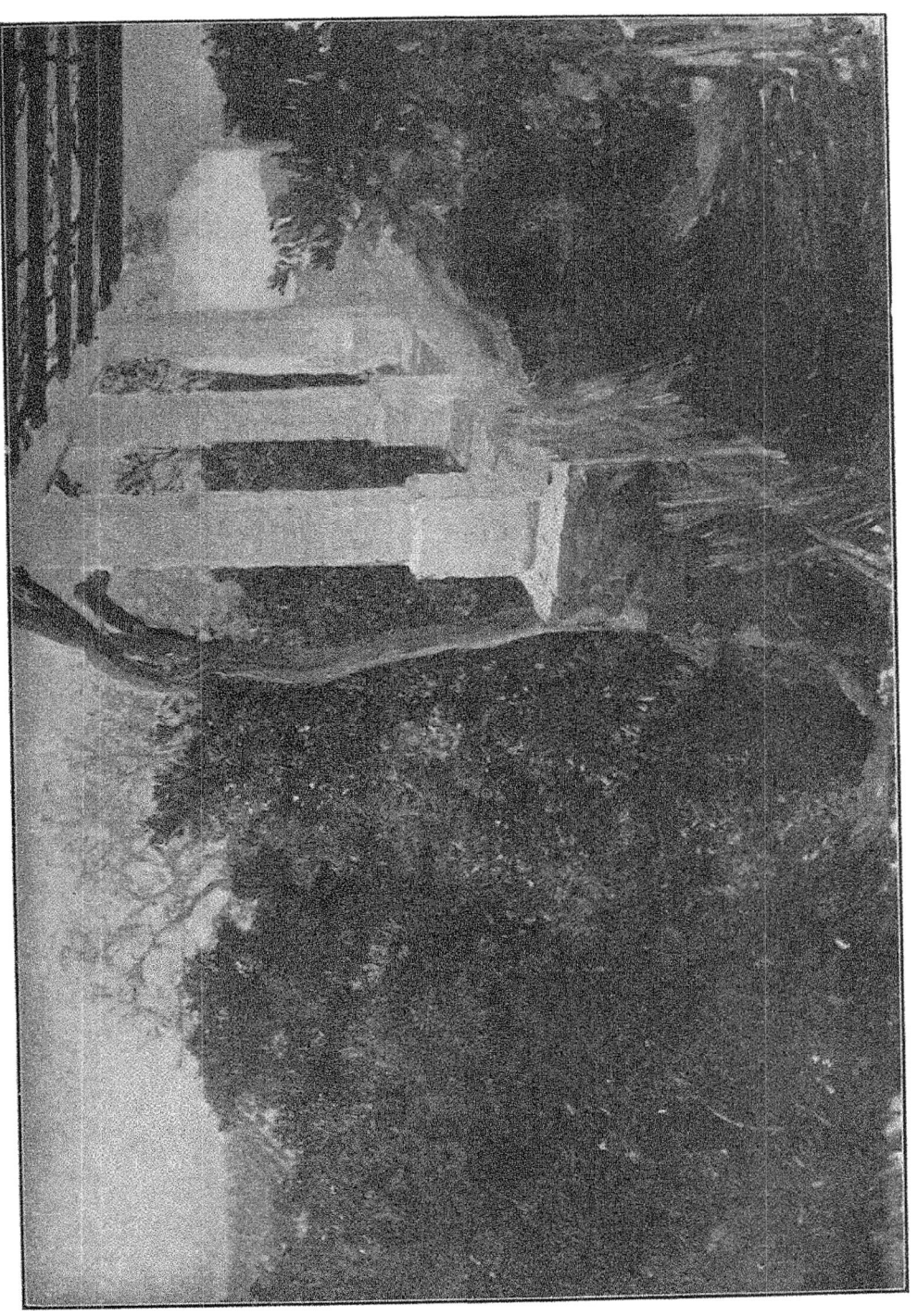

14

tic School, much of whose influence is, however, noticeable in the work of Ferrant, Elbo, Esquivel, Tejeo, Jenaro Pérez Villaamıl, and Gutiérrez de la Vega.

These men were very mediocre artists, but one of them, Jenaro Pérez Villaamil, possessed a comical and striking personality. He styled himself a landscape-painter, and professed to teach this subject at the National Academy of Art. Nevertheless, as Martin Rico tells us in his entertaining Memoir, the members of Jenaro's class were not allowed on any terms to stray into the open air. Each of them was immured within a small and feebly lighted room, together with his requisite materials and a pile of lithograph reproductions of the old Dutch masters. From these the student picked a fragment here and there, combined these elements as best he could into the semblance of a drawing, applied a coat or two of color, and handed in the whole concoction as a natural and harmonious landscape.

The methods of Jenaro Pérez Villaamil himself were no less singular. He seldom uttered any eriti cism to his flock, but sometimes took a brush and lighted up their lurid labors by the introduction of a fancy sunset. His own were executed in the following manner: gathering a lump of sepia, indigo,

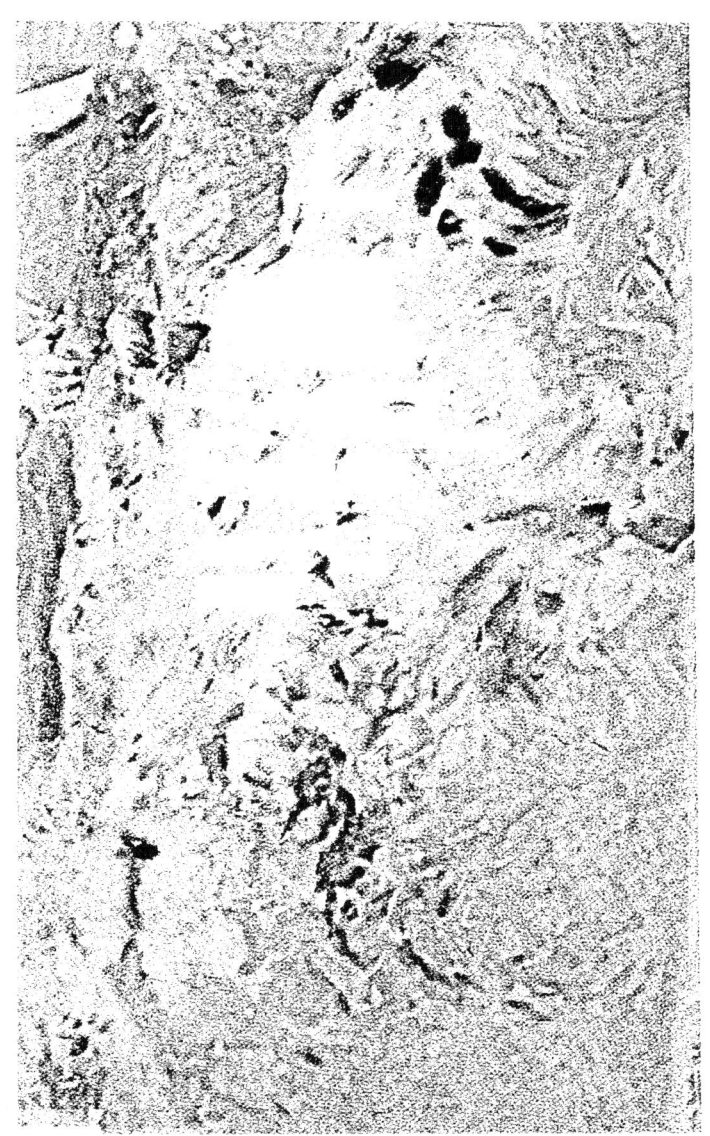

orange, or some other color, on his palette-knife, he dabbed it on the center of his canvas; and from this blot, says Martin Rico, "there would immediately appear a range of mountains, a cascade, a forest, or a cavern full of brigands. He gave me, I remember, one of these productions. It purported to represent a cross upon a rock, such as is often met with on the roads of Spain, and underneath he placed the sinister description, 'In this spot a man was murdered.' "

A false romanticism of this kind begets a fashion for the futile painting of dead history. Such was the case toward this time in the Peninsula. The principal leader of this movement, which attained its crisis in or about the year 1860, was Federico Madrazo (1815–94), the son of José Madrazo, and influenced, through his father, by the Frenchman David. The young Madrazo's style, while markedly eclectic as a whole, inclined at certain moments to the realism of Velazquez. Had he been born a little later, his work would have endured; but as it was, he and his age alike combined to neutralize each other in the world of art. Their baneful influence was inherently and unavoidably reciprocal.

Madrazo was an indefatigable and self-sacrificing teacher. Among his long array of pupils were Casado del Alisal (1831–86), Rosales (1836–73), and Martin Rico, who, though of an advanced age, is still living. This artist, who departed very widely from the theories and precepts of his master, is celebrated for his rendering of Spanish landscape, such as the snow-clad prospects of the Guadarrama, or romantic nooks and crannies of Castile or Andalusia. "Few painters," says a Spanish critic, "have hitherto expressed with such convincing power the effects of sunlight falling on our gardens or our towers, or on the scutcheons and the window-gratings of our ancient palaces."

Casado was a dexterous painter of bad subjects; that is, of bygone history no longer serviceable to the eye of modern art. His best-known works, such as "The Battle of Bailén," "The Comuneros of Castile," "The Last Moments of King Ferdinand the Summoned," or "The Cortes Taking the Oath at Cádiz," fail to attract us at this day, not from deficient treatment, but because they represent no phase of history painted, as all history must be painted, from the actual and contemporary scene. A similar judgment must be passed upon Rosales, author, among a quantity of other paintings, of "Hamlet and Ophelia," "The Death of Lucretia," "Isabella the Catholic Dictating her Will," and "The Presenting of Don

Juan de Austria to the Emperor Charles the Fifth."
Rosales had a fine spontaneous gift for rendering
light and shadow in the mass by leaving out unneces-
sary detail; but he died too early to mature the native
talent which endowed him in a generous degree.
Had he been spared awhile, the realistic and reac-
tionary movement which was only just beginning at
his death, would probably have reclaimed his vision
from the vain pursuit of buried and forgotten ages
to the profitable contemplation of a living world.[1]

The reaction in favor of realism which began to
show itself in Spain precisely at the moment when
the painting of dead history was in a manifest de-
cline, was principally due to the tuition and example
of one single artist. This was the landscape-painter
Charles Haes (1831–98), who, though a Belgian by
birth, had made his lifelong residence in the Peninsula. No field could have been better suited to his
labor, since the Spaniards heretofore had represented
natural scenery so very rarely that prior to the middle
of the nineteenth century only four—Mazo, Collan
tes, Brambilla, and Montalvo—had practised land-

[1] Fortuny does not need to be included with this group of
Spanish painters. The character of his art is French, and
though he was born in Cataluña, it has been justly said of him
that he was "educated outside Spain, lived outside Spain, flour-
ished outside Spain, and died outside Spain."

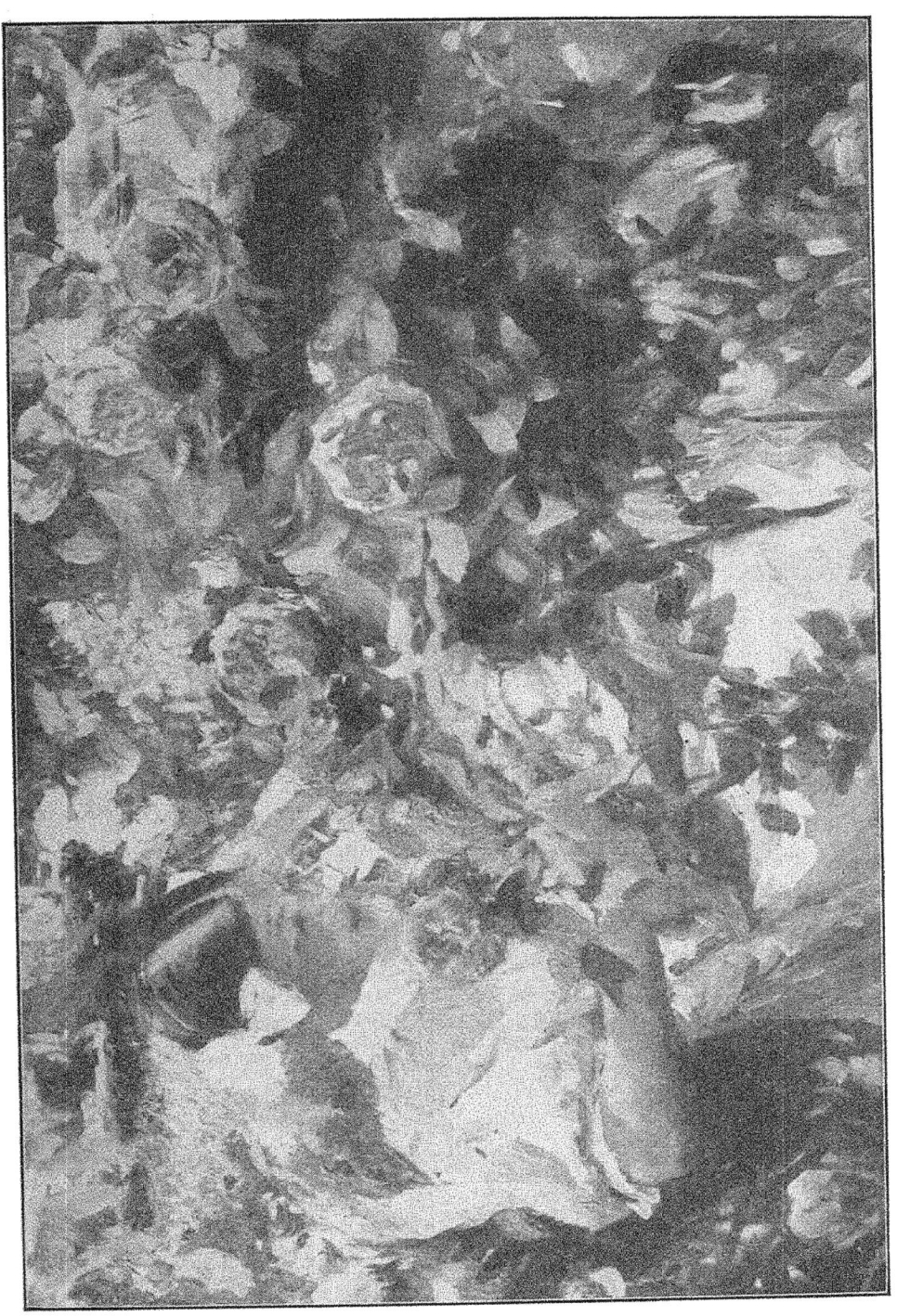

scape-painting as a self-contained and definite branch of art.[1]

The classes of Charles Haes were opened at Madrid in 1856. As in the case of most reformers, the outset of his errand was ungrateful. His pupils, though attracted by his patient courtesy, laughed at his landscapes scrupulously painted from the open air, while they themselves, without a condescending glance at Nature's self, composed, in the kaleidoscopic manner of Pérez Villaamil, "impossible flights of orange-colored scenery, studded with imaginary castles." Yet this was only for a while. Presently

[1] Collantes and Brambilla are of slight account as artists. Bartolomé Montalvo (1769-1846) was not much better. Collantes (1599-1656) was a pupil of Vicente Carducho, and painted figures and still-life, as well as pure landscape.

Juan Bautista Martinez del Mazo, who merits a higher rank among the older Spanish masters than he actually holds, was born at Madrid toward the year 1600, and died in the same city in 1667. He was the favorite and most gifted pupil of Velazquez, whose daughter, Doña Francisca, he married. In addition to his landscapes, which are relieved occasionally by the introduction of animated and attractive groups of figures, he copied Titian and Rubens in so masterly a manner that these copies have often been mistaken for, or wilfully passed off as, the originals.

The Prado Gallery contains Mazo's excellent "View of the City of Saragossa," a work which is enlivened by a multitude of figures sitting or standing, and conversing. Probably some of these were executed or completed by Velazquez, who chanced to visit Saragossa precisely at the time when Mazo was engaged upon the painting.

the manifest sincerity of Haes, together with the no less manifest and truthful power of his doctrine, won over a continually increasing section, both of his pupils and of the wider public. Work of his own, such as the noble prospects of the "Cerro Coronado" and the "Peña de los Enamorados," as well as that of two or three who studied under him, attracted much attention at the series of biennial exhibitions which had recently been organized in the capital of Spain. A genuine and deep-seated sympathy with realism declared itself in every phase of Spanish art. Even the painters of dead history were touched by it, and aimed at better coloring and better composition, or else, more wisely still, forsook their arid ground and struck aside into the fertile fields of portraiture and landscape.

This was about the time when the Pre-Raphaelites in England and the Impressionists in France were almost simultaneously beginning to be known. Happily for Spain, the fallacies of our British Brotherhood were never wafted to her shore. Not so, however, with Impressionism, which has affected Spanish painting in a sensible degree, though somewhat locally. Toward the concluding quarter of the nineteenth century, the influence of the French *plein airiste* group extended into Cataluña, where the respective styles of Rousseau, Diaz, Millet, Courbet, and Corot were zealously reflected by the painters Baixeras, Planella, Pellicer, Mercadé, Sans, Fabrés, Urgell, and Vayreda.

Nevertheless, this change was eminently for the good of the Peninsula. Hitherto the merest appanage of France, she now regained her own volition, and began to be once more herself. Sorolla, González Bilbao, Rusiñol, Meifren, Mir, and Plá among her painters; Blay, Benlliure, and Querol among her sculptors—these and many others are the virile artist-offspring of a hopeful and rejuvenated Spain, who cleared from before her eyes the mists of antiquated prejudice, and newly looked about her unto life. Not only at Madrid, but in a nucleus of the provinces, and thence, by rapid and successive impulses, throughout the greater portion of the land, such artists, stimulated, like all other classes of the Spaniards, by this fortunate awakening, busied themselves to render in a natural, unidealized, and unacademic form, the manifold customs and emotions of her laborer, artisan, and peasant people. The painters Fierros Plasencia, Souto, Uria, Silvio Fernández, Pradilla, and Martinez Abades in Galicia and Asturias; Moreno Carbonero, Blanco Coris, Villegas, and Garcia Ramos in Andalusia; Cebrián, Senent, Albert, Mezquita, Leonar, and Amorós in Valencia—deserve the principal credit of this movement. So that, in modern Spanish art, the landscape and the rural or bucolic styles were twin productions of a little later than the middle of the nineteenth century, and were associated by a brotherly intimacy. Part of their character was assimilated from a foreign source. The other part is traceable, through Goya and the general line of Spanish realism, to Velazquez.

Thus there had come to pass, originating, at a lapse of more than half a century, from the blunt, uncompromising realism of Francisco Goya, a vigorous, wide-reaching, and successful agitation to revive the style of rustic genre. Though not the first in literal priority, Sorolla is undoubtedly the first in rank and consequence of the initiators of this movement. His industry endowed their efforts with a vital and enduring force. His genius was the oriflamme that led them on to victory. His art, at once original and national, assisted, by its technical and spiritual grandeur, to remove their need of foreign tutelage, fixing the proper middle-line between the riot of Impressionism and the lethargy of routine, reading the glorious nature-truth for good and all, and manifesting to the world innumerable excellencies of the scenery and customs of contemporary Spain

Sincerity and actuality and sympathy—here are the qualities which make Sorolla's renderings of Spanish life at once so beautiful and so robust, establishing our belief that not only are they of vital interest now, but of a value which shall palpitate in far futurity. All painting that is truly great depends infallibly upon the interaction of two kinds of power in the artist. The one kind is the moral, intellectual, and emotional power resulting from sincerity and actuality and sympathy: the other is the manual and material power of technique. The power of the heart creates and is created by the power of the hand. Not otherwise have the privileged heart and hand combined to form and animate the art of Joaquin Sorolla.

In the domain of art, sincerity, although related to, is not identical with sympathy. It is a less exalted gift, bearing a close affinity to conscientiousness. Many a painter is sincere, who is not also sympathetic. Even the sincerest seeker after truth may be mistaken in his quest. The form he finds may be conventional, supposititious truth, wearing the guise of truth by some impertinent misnomer. But sympathy points forward to the undivided truth; points to a vital

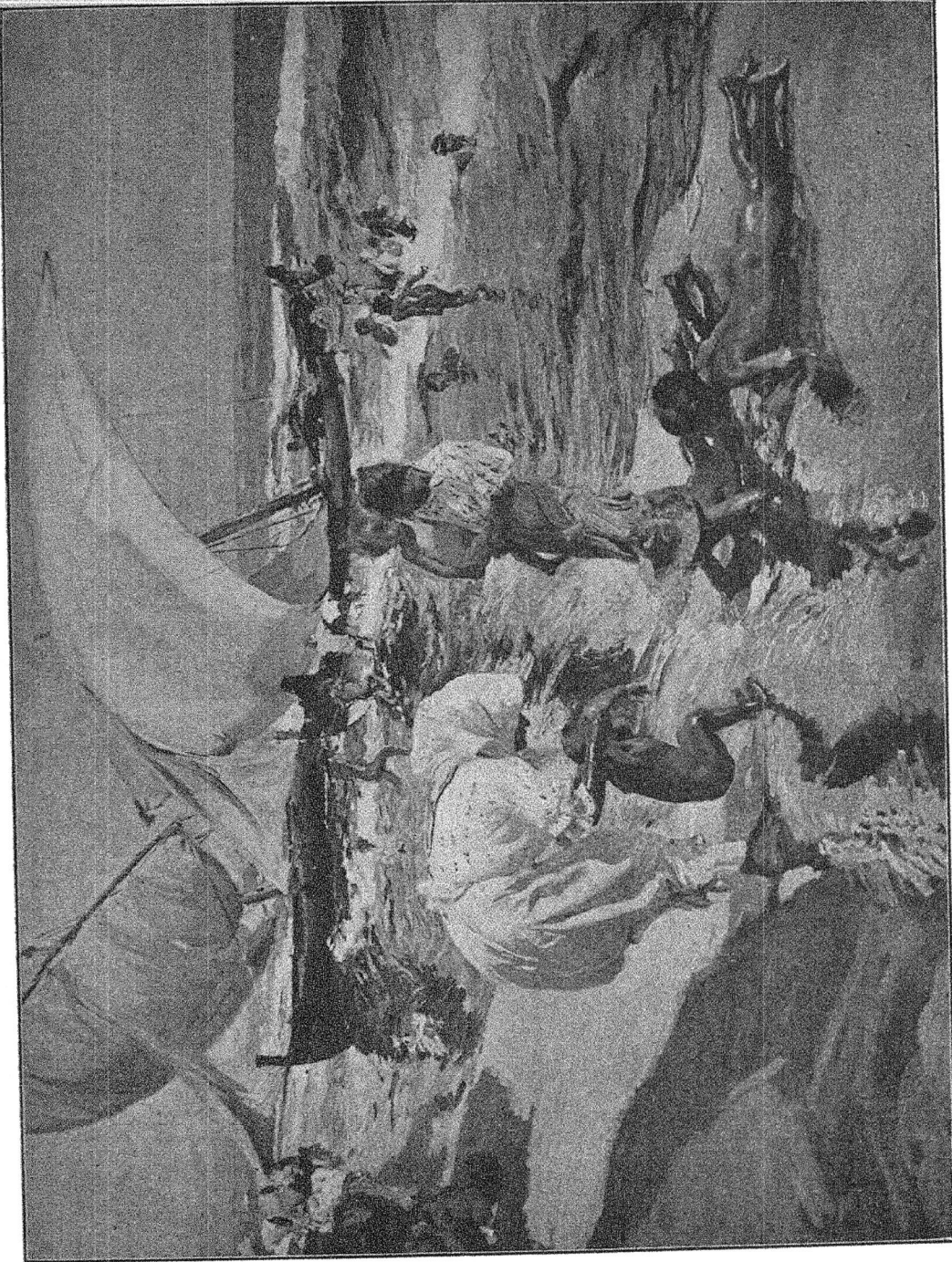

figure, not a shadow; not to artifice, but natural emotion. Duty alone may prompt sincerity, but sympathy in its genuine form is traceable to genius. True sympathy has more prevision than sincerity. Mere sincerity implies dependence on another; but thorough sympathy is strong enough to stand alone. And when, attended by technique and actuality, sincerity and sympathy combine, then the result is not a fractionary, latent, or inactive, but a perfect, potent, and amazingly creative genius.

I copy *in extenso* Ruskin's words on actuality in painting; which words, though undeservedly included with his indefensible defense of the Pre-Raphaelites, are in themselves closely expressive of the truth. "What do you at present *mean*," he asked, "by historical painting? Nowadays, it means the endeavoring, by the power of imagination, to portray some historical event of past days. But in the middle ages, it meant representing the acts of *their* own days; and that is the only historical painting worth a straw. Of all the wastes of time and sense which modernism has invented—and they are many—none are so ridiculous as this endeavor to represent past history. What do you suppose our descendants will care for our imaginations of the events of former days? Suppose the Greeks, instead of representing

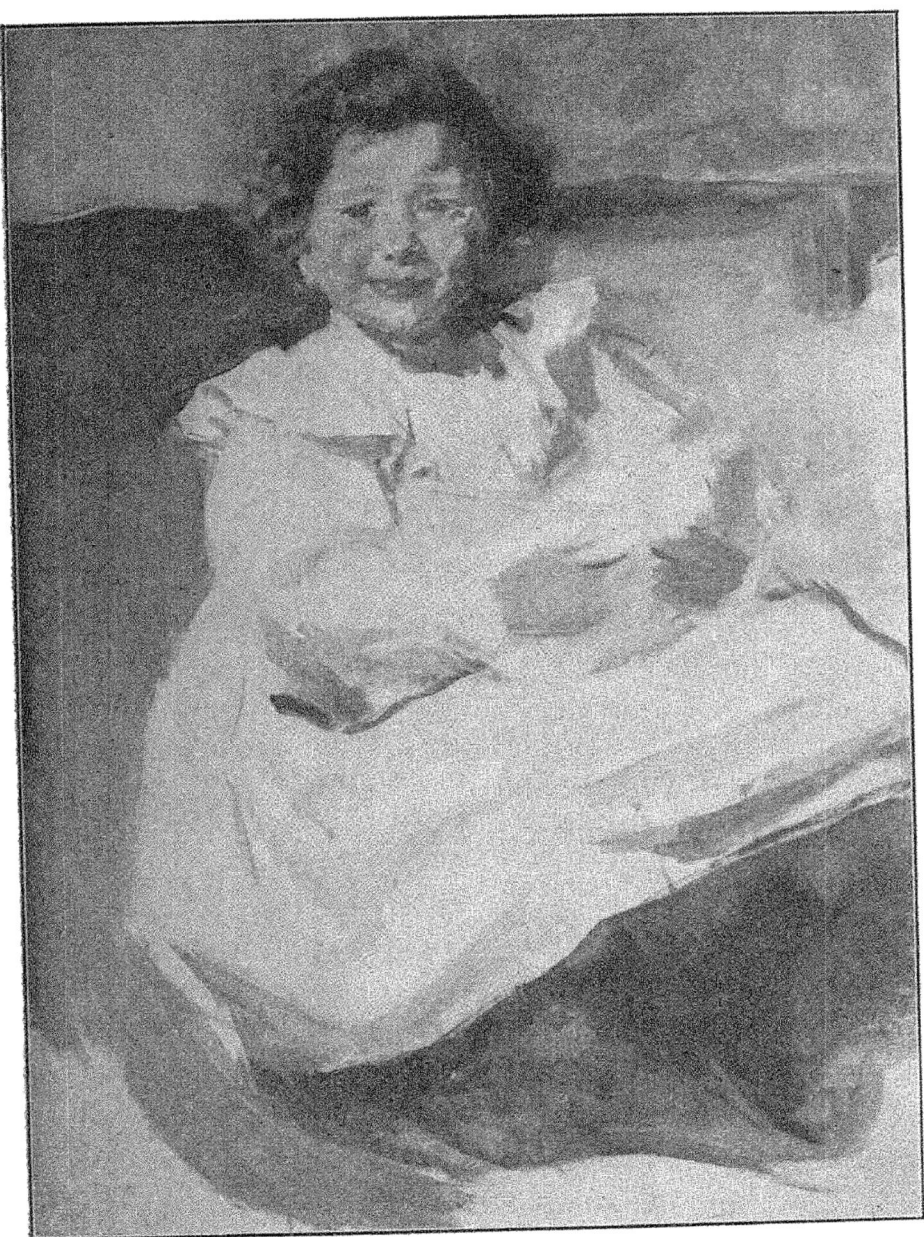

their own warriors as they fought at Marathon, had left us nothing but their imaginations of Egyptian battles; and suppose the Italians, in like manner, instead of portraits of Can Grande and Dante, or of Leo the Tenth and Raphael, had left us nothing but imaginary portraits of Pericles and Miltiades? What fools we should have thought them! how bitterly we should have been provoked with their folly! And that is precisely what our descendants will feel towards us, so far as our grand historical and classical schools are concerned. What do we care, they will say, what those nineteenth-century people fancied about Greek and Roman history! If they had left us a few plain and rational sculptures and pictures of their own battles, and their own men, in their everyday dress, we should have thanked them. Well, but, you will say, we *have* left them portraits of our great men, and paintings of our great battles. Yes, you have indeed, and that is the only historical painting that you either have, or can have; but you don't *call* that historical painting. . . As you examine into the career of historical painting, you will be more and more struck with the fact I have this evening stated to you,—that none was ever truly great but that which represented the living forms and daily deeds of the people among whom it arose;—that all precious historical work records, not the past, but the present."

Spain is above all other lands the land of realists; that is, in art, of painters of the actual. From first to last the life-work of Velazquez, which consists of portraits, landscapes,[1] genre, and renderings of so called mythological or sacred subjects, is real and therefore actual. It is completely and consistently non-retrospective, non-archaic. All of it is truthfully to be defined as portraiture, using this term, not in the circumscribed and ordinary sense, but as it was pointed out by Bastien-Lepage, who wisely said, "I believe that everything in nature, even a tree, even still-life, should be treated *as a portrait.*" For so it is, a portrait; and all painting is, or should be, portraiture.

Velazquez had no speculation for the past. His eye and genius were in sympathy with his age alone. His only scope was portraiture. His canvases display

[1] The landscapes and the landscape-backgrounds of Velazquez are not only sovereign and insuperable in technique, but absolutely sympathetic, actual, and unconventional. Together with a thousand other paintings by the older masters, they constitute a crushing refutation of that "irresponsible and dogmatic" phrase by Ruskin—"None before Turner had lifted the veil from the face of nature; the majesty of the hills and forests had received no interpretation, and the clouds passed unrecorded from the face of the heaven which they adorned, and of the earth to which they ministered."

to us the manifold component characters of his century. His Christ and his Madonna, his Æsop and Menippus, his Mars, and Mercury, and Vulcan, are simply, and despite their fanciful appellations, Spaniards of his very time; not fictions simulated from past history, but facts proceeding from the native circumstances of his own. His Christ is not heroic and gigantic, in the muscular, mythologizing style of Michelangelo; not a conventional embodiment of virtue, but the actual figure of a man.

Closely akin to actuality is swiftness. Protracted workmanship in painting violates the triple truth of light and shade and atmosphere. All beings and all things whose aspect, as our vision apprehends them, is effected by the vivifying influence of the sun or moon, change in that aspect from one fraction of each instant to the fraction following. Their constant state is not stagnation but vibration. Their symbol is a point and not a line. Therefore the painter needs to catch their infinite transitions with an infinite rapidity; to render, by the limited means at his command, unlimited variety; and, by accomplishing the maximum of technical exactness with the minimum expenditure of time, by one endeavor to achieve a twofold conquest.

In every artist of true capability, this power of

swiftness was existent at his birth, though further and assiduous discipline alone can strengthen him to seize and to retain those evanescent and elusive semblances in nature. The secret of all realism, all "impression ism" proper, is contained in this—the very same which is unfolded by the early realists in splendid and imperious silence, and subsequently, in a clamorous and ostentatious fashion, by the modern French Impressionists. Sorolla, who proclaims it quietly and nobly in his painting, in our familiar talk assures me that its knowledge beat within him at all moments, just as rhythmical and constant as the beatings of his heart. "It came to me," he says, "together with my earliest sympathy with nature. My studies in the open air cannot admit of lengthy execution. I feel that if I painted slowly, I positively could not paint at all."

All painters who have painted slowly have produced their labor at a sacrifice of atmosphere and natural truth. The finest atmosphere in all the world of painting is the background of the "Las Meninas" of Velazquez, which is reproductive of a natural and accustomed depth of gloom. Examining this background through a lens, we find Velazquez to have moved his brush, charged with thin color, in a swift and spacious sweep. The coating is diaphanous throughout. The very texture of the canvas is not smothered up, but utilized to convey the semblance of tenuity.

Sympathy promotes and regulates the artist's sense of value. Much error has been propagated in this matter of artistic values. "All things," protested Courbet, in reply to certain of his critics, "are of an equal value to the painter." Here lurks a pseudo-truism. All things are not of equal value unto nature's self. This is precisely where the painter must be able to discriminate. In nature and, by consequence, in art, the value of all objects is not constant, but fluctuating; not homogeneous, but diverse. All things, as Ruskin pointed out, are "coexistent and yet separate." No absolute isolation is conceivable in nature. A spear, a plant, a tree, a piece of clothing any object that you please—has its particular value, and again, that other value which accrues to it from casual or intended circumstances. Its incidental or premeditated neighborhood to other objects modifies these values by contributing to them other and contingent values. These supplementary and complex values, interacting with its very own, affect it as to form and color, history, locality, and even ethics. In "The Surrender of Breda," by Velazquez, the row of lances have their quasi-isolated or particular value, yet affect, and are affected by, the episode of which they are a factor. They intercept the sky, and influence, and are influenced by, the shades and values of that sky. Again, these formidable weapons of Biscayan ash possess a martial and historic interest. Their shape and length denote a certain moment in the annals of their native country. Who shall in consequence pretend that, as they tremble in the hands of living and victorious soldiery, they have the same significance and value as a row of lances represented all alone?

Sympathy prompts the painter to discern and extricate these values that exist and subexist in nature. While yet his composition as to color, shape, and context must be nature's own, his system must be happily though truthfully selective; must be apposite and opportune, as well as natural. It is by no means unimportant whether his subjects meet our eye in such a disposition or in such another one; whether their moods, as he conveys them to our ken, be regular or fitful, grave or gay, serene or agitated. The robes of cardinals are red; but in one famous portrait such a robe accentuates the *sanguin .; y* instincts of a certain cardinal whose ferocity upset the peace of nations. That robe contains at once a general and a special symbolism. Its color overspreads the character of the wearer in relation to a certain phase of history. So, both in nature and in art, the circumstances which invest a person or a thing are often as significant as, or more significant than, that person or that thing considered in a state of quasi-isolation.

Sympathy, which endows our thoughts and actions with a superadded life, also endows the painter's canvas with a superadded vital power. It makes him conscious of the soul, alike of persons and of things, as well as of their outer and apparent form. Unsympathetic painters are precluded from a perfect greatness. For only sympathy is able to perceive the spiritual beauty in its actual and true relation to the carnal. The ugliness or beauty of a human being proceeds, not from the essence or the form alone, but from the subtle interaction of the two. This inner and this outer symmetry or ugliness are never disassociated. The relatively perfect human beauty is the union of both symmetries; the relatively perfect human ugliness, the union of both opposites of symmetry. An outer symmetry may yet accompany a crooked soul, or else, as in the "Portrait of an Old Man with a Bulbous Nose," by Ghirlandajo, a want of outer symmetry may be transfigured by a psychic sweetness—by the spiritual symmetry—into a pleas ing semblance that is almost physically beautiful. It was remarked by Bastien-Lepage that "most of Hol

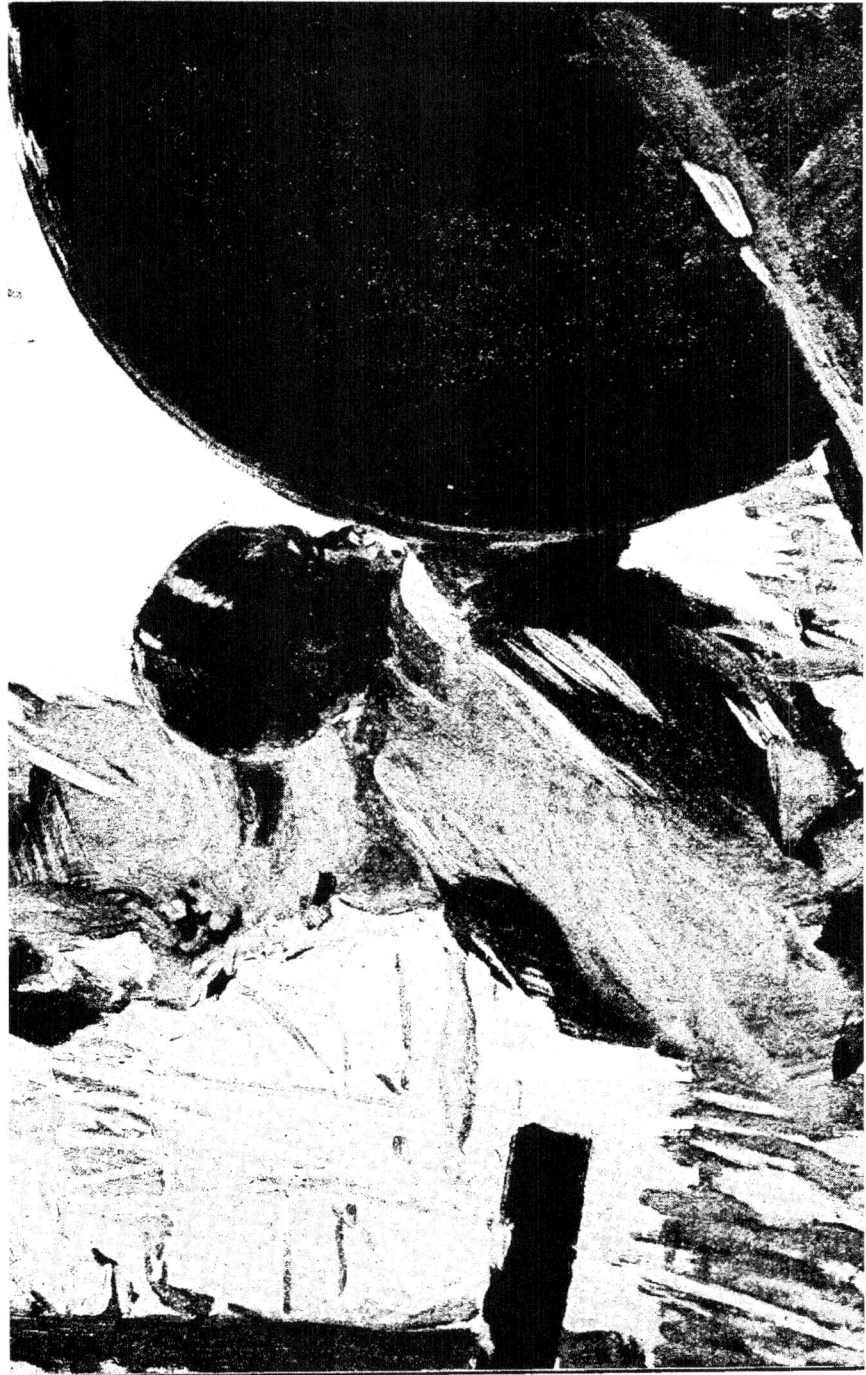

bein's heads are not beautiful in the plastic sense of the word, but none the less they are singularly interesting. For, underneath their very ugliness and vulgarity, we find the thought and feeling that glorifies everything. The peasant, he, too, has his fashion of being sad or joyous, of feeling and of thinking. It is that particular fashion which we must try to discover. When you have found out and represented *that,* it matters little if your personages have irregular features, clumsy manners, and coarse hands. They cannot fail to be beautiful because they will be living and thinking beings. The patient, conscientious study of nature—that is the only thing worth having."

The love of truth is normally inherent in mankind; but few of us—alas, how very few—are able to distinguish her unaided. For truth is not self-evident, as most of us believe, but complex and recondite. Prejudice and routine have largely veiled her from our eyes. Our vision and our reasoning alike partake of this deficiency. Speaking of painters in particular, "It is most difficult," said Ruskin, "and worthy of the greatest men's greatest effort, to render, as it should be rendered, the simplest of the natural features of the earth." And not alone such features, but everything that is a fact. So that the great historian, poet, novelist, or philosopher in his writings, the great sculptor in his statues, and the great painter in his canvases, make us acquainted with the truth by guiding us into her temple. Their sympathy evokes our own. Their genius wakes and fortifies our dormant sensibility. Chosen high-priests of nature in themselves, their ministry and devotion elevate us also into conscious and devoted worshipers.

In spite of all its faults, this age of ours is predisposed to search whole-heartedly for truth. Yet we are spoiled by one infirmity. Nerves are the cause of nearly all our recent disabilities. Such is our inborn aim, and yet our nerves resist and thwart us in the consummation of this aim. For all our aspirations and investigations after truth, we are a generation that is preyed upon by nervous weakness. As if in our infirm belief we soared too far above the common earth to discipline our earthly constitution, our politics and state-craft, our morals and our acts, are handicapped by neurasthenia. Problems of sovereign issue, such as the social or political relations of the woman to the man, of capital to labor, wealth to poverty, inventive effort to executive, the veto of the state upon intemperance, or ignorance, or sloth— engage and interest us hourly. It is our honest and collective aim to grapple with these arduous and ambitious problems; but then, like the maleficent sprite escaping from Pandora's fabled casket, the demon of our nerves assails us with invisible shafts and robs us of our victory.

Among the past or present victims of this demon we must count the masters and disciples of Pre-Raphaelitism one and all, and nearly all the French Impressionists. Their nature is not healthy, neither is their painting. "In art," observed the Spaniard Ganivet, "the logical is *always* superior to the allegorical." This truth was veiled from the Pre-Raphaelites. Their view of life was either fanciful and meaningless, or retrospective; and it is obvious that, when we seek to disinter the past, we work with borrowed eyes and ears. "Every great man," said Ruskin, in a lucid and deliberate passage of his writings, "paints what he sees or did see, his greatness being indeed little else than his intense sense of fact." Therefore Pre-Raphaelistic painting has no sense of fact; since, for the sympathetic painter, every fact is of his moment, visible and actual.

A healthy sympathy with art is not to be discovered in our medievalizing Brotherhood, or (in the large majority of cases) in the prestidigitation of impressionizing Frenchmen. Yet good example may create itself out of the ashes of the evil. Painting in England has advanced but lamely from the ruins of Pre-

326

Raphaelitism toward a better goal; while, on the other hand, in France, the saner masters of Impressionism —notably Renoir, Pissaro, Sisley, and Degas—have opportunely redirected modern art toward those primitive and reticent "Impressionists" who led their privileged and prolific lives before the troubled days of modern neurasthenia.

No prey to nervous weakness is Sorolla; neither was Bastien-Lepage. There is a splendid sympathy between these two—between the peasant-realist of modern France and the peasant-realist of modern Spain. I make no effort to compare them critically. It is a dangerous and often sterile labor, with respect to art, to pry about in order to determine influences. Influence in art is to a vast extent fortuitous. Few painters can themselves explain its origin. "I have no fixed rules and no particular method," pleaded Jules Bastien-Lepage; "I paint things just as I see them, sometimes in one fashion, sometimes in another, and afterward *I hear people say that they are like Rembrandt or like Clouet.*" Influence in art is conscious, or unconscious, or subconscious. Who shall, in any given case, definitively separate the three? A chance inspection of a print or drawing brought by Fortune's fingers from Japan, may have affected the entire work of Whistler, and hence, through Whistler, much, or possibly the whole, of recent art. Strong in the mass, the web of life is spun from infinitely tiny strands. A gradual or abrupt accretion of coincidences is the groundwork of all progress; and what was yesterday an isolated accident, to-day is an absorbing purpose.

And so, to state the simple truth, Joaquin Sorolla and Jules Bastien-Lepage are just two parallel examples of extraordinary peasant-genius. Their early circumstances were the same. We read of Bastien-Lepage, "His parents were poor, and he had to make his own way in the world." Again, "At home or at school, he was always drawing, on the margin of his lesson-books, on the doors and walls." And again, "His native courage and good spirits, together with that invincible tenacity of purpose which was so marked a feature of his character, stood him in good stead, and helped him through the trials and difficulties of the next few years." These very sentences are applicable to Sorolla. Both of these men unite a peasant's vision with immense interpretative genius. They are at once sincere and actual, profoundly sympathetic, mighty masters of technique. Their view is not deflected by the neurasthenia of overculture. They do not strain to found a blatant sect or school, to disinter past mannerisms, to make themselves con-

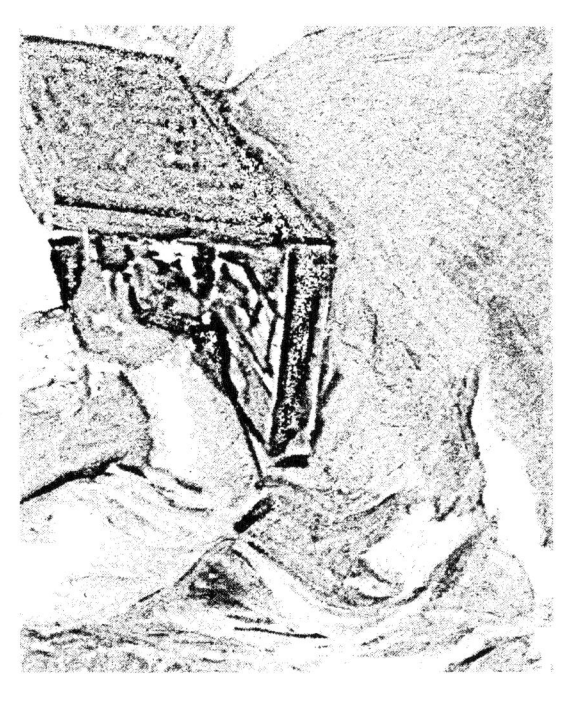

spicuous by a novel idiocrasy; but to be Nature's servitors alone, and by this sacrifice to minister to her glory.

They are apart from, and superior to, the modern French "Impressionists." Their art is healthier, more spontaneous, and more earnest. They are the older-fashioned and the purer species of Impressionist—that is, the simple realist. They are a new Teniers, a new Velazquez, a new Goya, a new Constable. They may appear, to the careless critic, to be innovators, but *are* positive descendants and direct continuators of an ancient and illustrious artist-line. And why, apart from by-considerations of technique, have they accomplished so unusual a triumph? To an immense extent, because the soundness of their peasant-nerves does not affect their retina adversely. They do not speculate or worry, but they see. Theirs is the peasant-influence that our modern world of art most needed. They are the very best corrective of our physical and social neurasthenia.

"In order to express," says Beruete, "the subtle yet intense vibrations of the sunlight, Sorolla sometimes uses crisp, small touches of the brush, though not in the extravagant fashion of the French Impressionists. He saw and speedily absorbed all that is healthy in the various phases of Impressionism; and so, in paint-

in all cases of consummate art, the *conscious* effort and the *conscious* pains were long precedent and preparatory to the fact, and therefore, when the latter stands before us in a perfect shape, the effort is, or seems to have become, subsensible.

An "infinite power of taking pains," and concentrating their effect in vast achievements which burst forth on our bewildered and delighted gaze as though they were unstudied and spontaneous, occurs but twice or thrice in any century. Nature, as it were, invests these rarely patient and perceptive characters with *her* facility and sureness, *her* puissance and fecundity. Such, as an artist, is Sorolla. His vision and his touch—"une main aussi prompte à peindre que le regard à percevoir"—identify their purpose to convey the pure interpretation of the truth. A spirit of herculean effort is absorbed into his very being, beating so close and constant that it is assimilated with a facile yet emotive spontaneity. "Il peint aussi naturellement qu'il parle, sans même se douter qu'il en puisse être autrement et que le tour de force per pétuel ne soit pas l'habitude de tout peintre." The difficult appears to succumb before the practice of surmounting difficulty. He is unconscious, through association, of the terrors of technique. The world exists for him twice over. He is at once the eye and

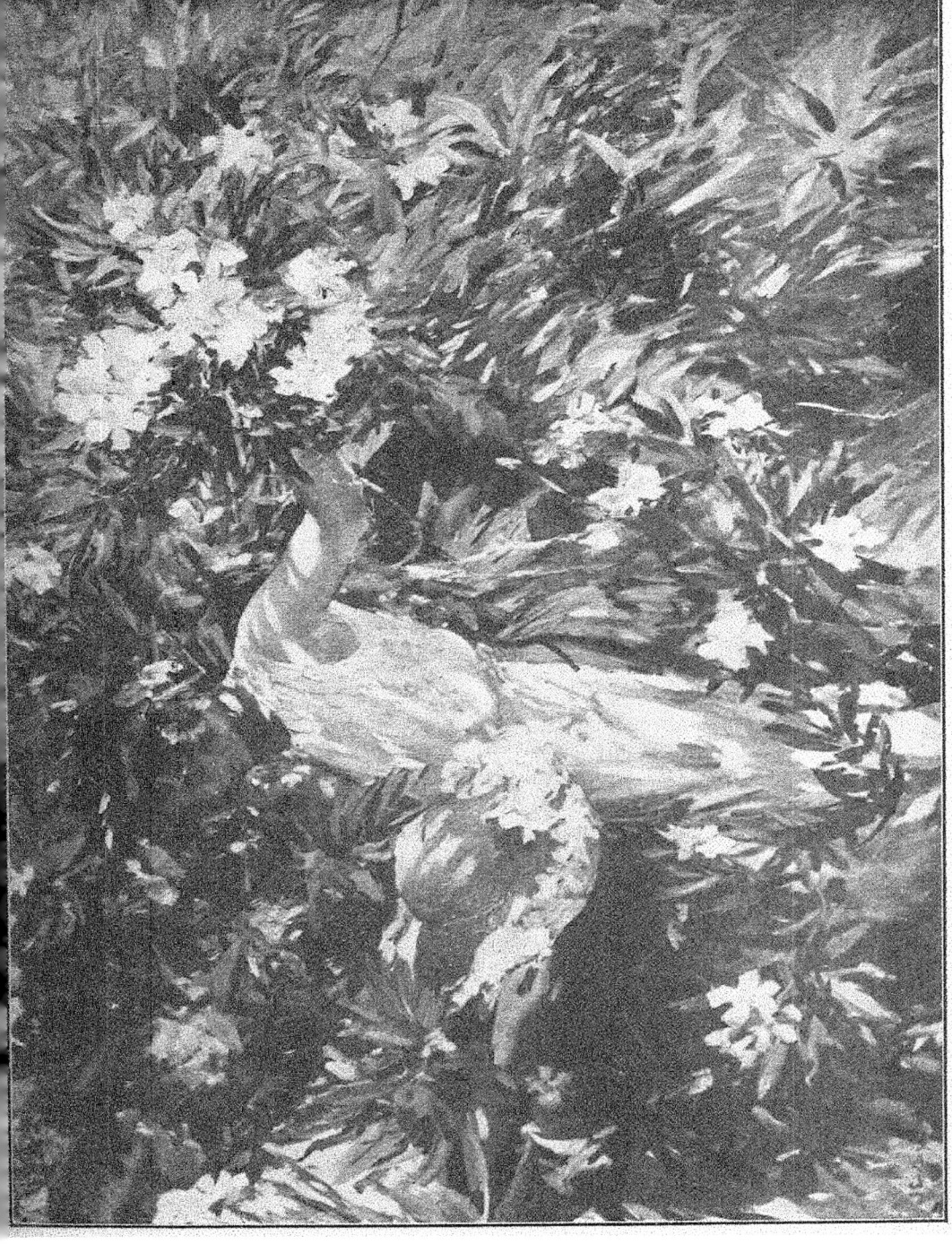

ing landscape, he banishes from his palette black or blackish, non-transparent colors, such as were formerly in vogue for rendering shadow. But, on the other hand, his canvases contain a great variety of blues and violets balanced and juxtaposed with reds and yellows. These, and the skilful use of white, provide him with a color-scheme of great simplicity, originality, and beauty."

A countryman of the Impressionists confirms this eulogy. Camille Mauclair has stated of Sorolla's painting, "On y trouve, à l'analyse, des qualités solides, une assise, un savoir, que bien peu d'impressionistes ont pu montrer dans leur art captivant mais vacillant, où la vibration chromatique trop souvent dévore les formes et détruit la stabilité de l'architecture du sol." He also comments on the swiftness of Sorolla's workmanship, of which he says, "L'éclat subit dissimule la longue préparation." *The lifelong preparation.* The truth is better indicated here than in this other sentence: "No great thing was ever done by great effort: a great thing can only be done by a great man, and he does it *without* effort." These latter words by Ruskin point a superficial aspect of the truth. Nothing at all in this world is accomplished without effort; and in proportion as the "thing" is worthy of achievement, so is the effort greater. But, hand of Nature, and his own. Although the strife takes place, it seems no longer arduous to strive; and yet infallibly to strive is to obtain.

Therefore no subject that exists in life, or in life's mirror, art, is too ambitious for Sorolla. Like an athlete outstripping every other in a race, he is unfaltering, unflagging, and supreme. He has no false direction to retrace, nothing whatever to unlearn; but has advanced from mastering slighter things to mastering the very greatest. His method is the undisguised and naked truth. Disdaining nugatory pointillism and the petulant *procédé de la tache,* he practises no legerdemain of daubs and dashes. Where color should be applied thinly, he applies it thinly, and where densely, densely; rendering, as it were, the natural technique of nature. What color is in actual life, such is Sorolla's coloring; and history, as she breathes to-day, will call to other generations from his canvas.

Children exulting in their pastime, girls with their skipping-rope, nude boys disporting in the sea, grown people of all ranks and occupations, from kings and queens in palaces to peasants pressing raisins in a shed, nobles and *caballeros* of unfurrowed countenance and creaseless clothing, ragged and rugged fishers, tanned to an equal brownness with their nets, the acts and the

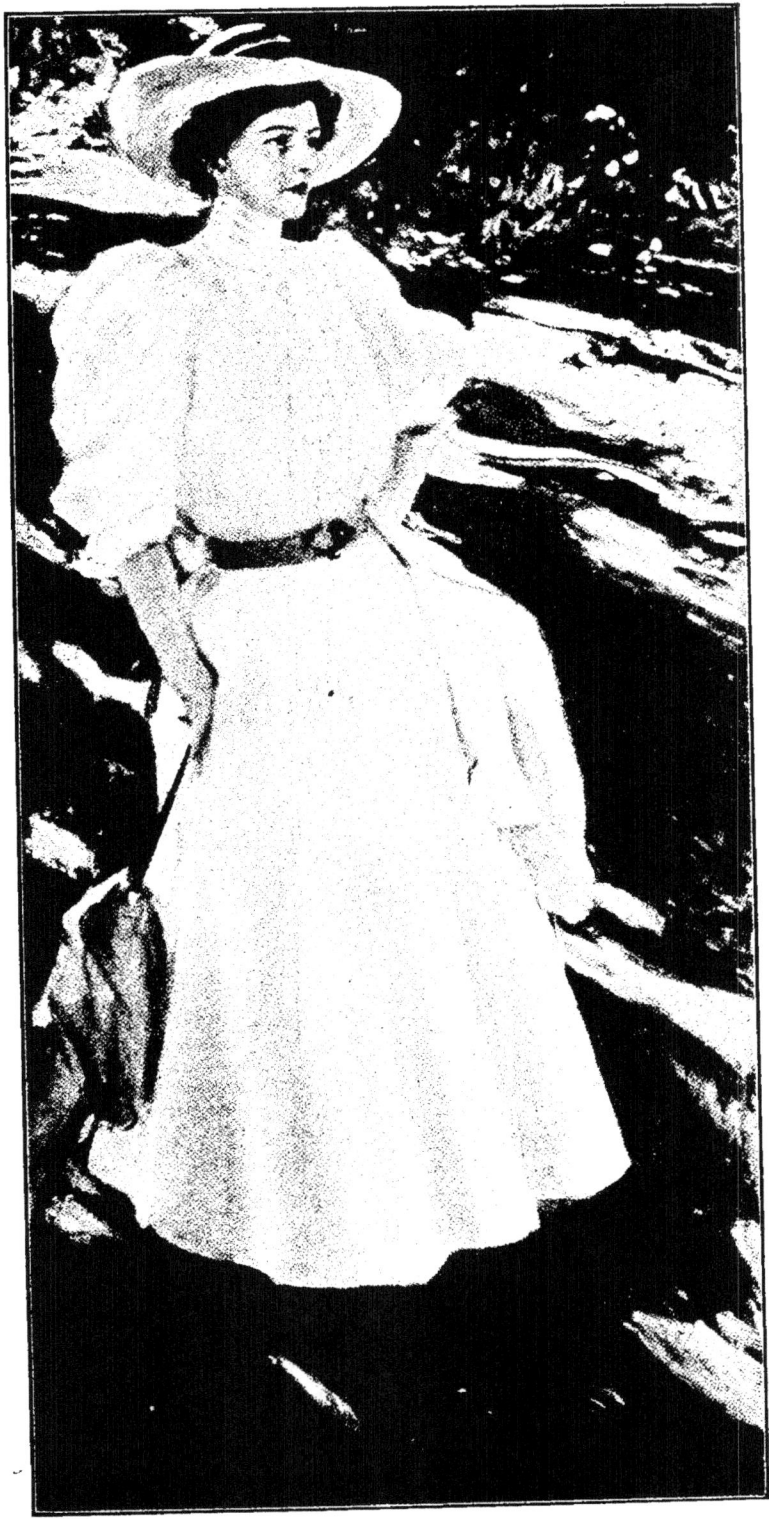

emotions of the coast or countryside, the placid harvest of the fields or perilous harvest of the deep, cattle of majestic stride that beach the boats or pasture in the glebe, subtle effects of air and light, the luminous gleam that filters through a sheet, a parasol, or a sail, the swaying of grass or boughs or draperies in the wind, zephyrs that wanton in a woman's hair or in the plumy foliage, the sprouting or declining leaves, umbrageous depths of forest, the stillness of still water, bellowing breakers, ripples that whisper over and caress the sand—Sorolla's genius has expressed them every one. "All of them pure veracities, therefore immortal." His loving industry confirmed and multiplied that genius. His diligent and loyal servitude to Nature reaped its due reward. Now she has elevated him beside herself, and crowns him with her own felicity.

Pre-Raphaelitism, medievalism, pointillism, chromatism; wilful and capricious lookings back or lookings forward; theory upon theory; fad upon fad—should all these sickly innovations be committed to the tomb, their loss will not affect us vitally. But alas for art when man should finally discard his interest in the life that is around, essential to, and interwoven with himself; when he should finally avert his eyes from fact to superstition; should hold in less than paramount

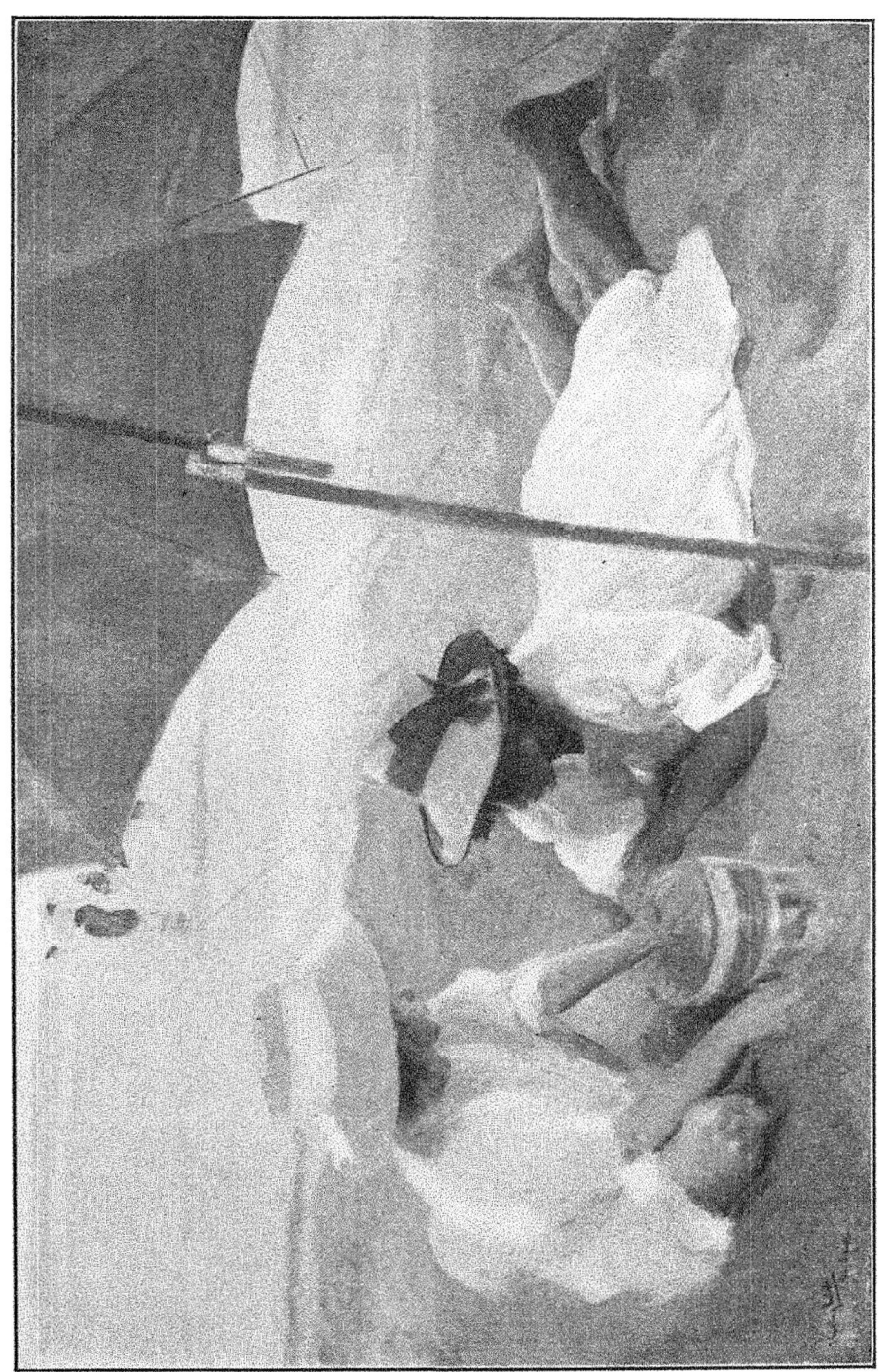

esteem the shape and soul of men and things, not as they might have been before, or may be after him, but as they bear him company between the actual limits of his birth and death. For this—the earnest, undivided study of his days alone—alone can yield him an approximated knowledge of the perfect truth; a noble privilege in answer to a noble quest; a triumph worthy to be chronicled by Progress on the purest and most lasting table of her golden archives.

LEONARD WILLIAMS.

CATALOGUE

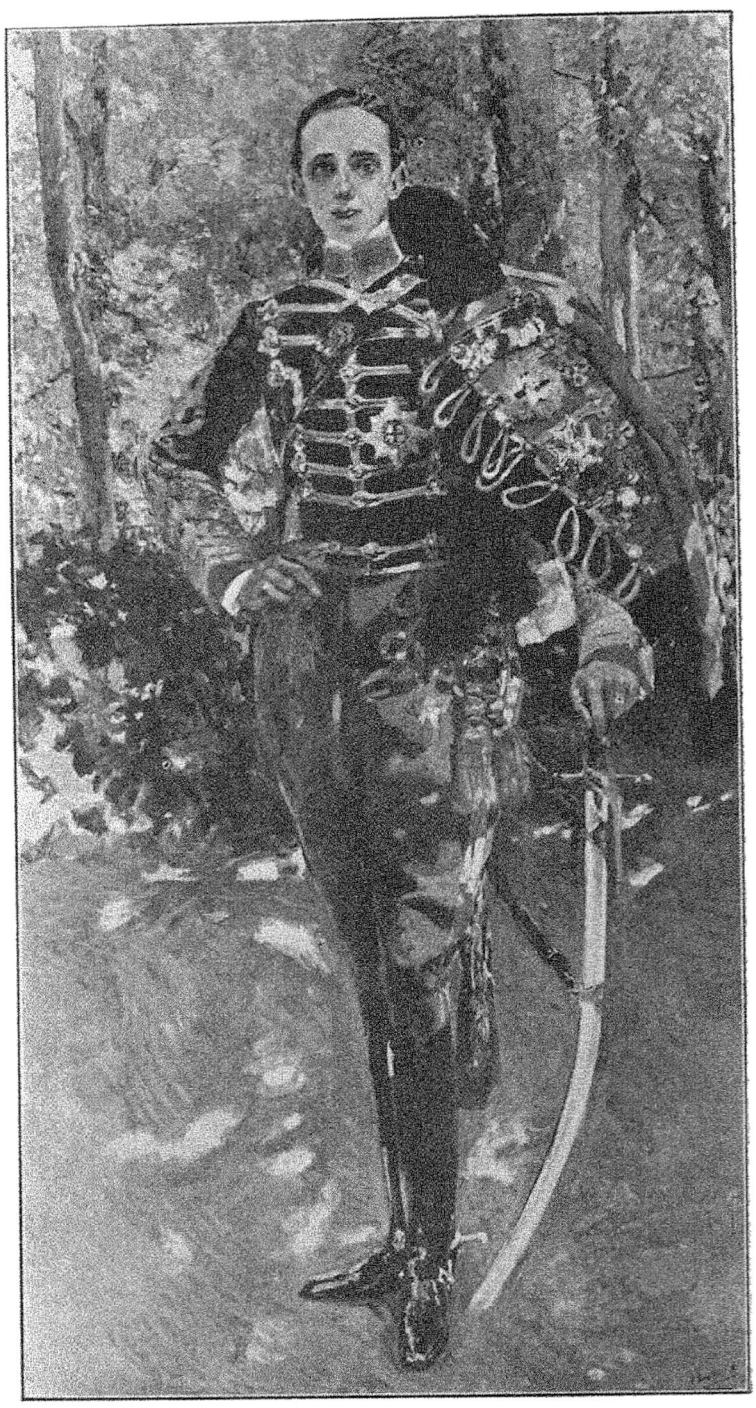

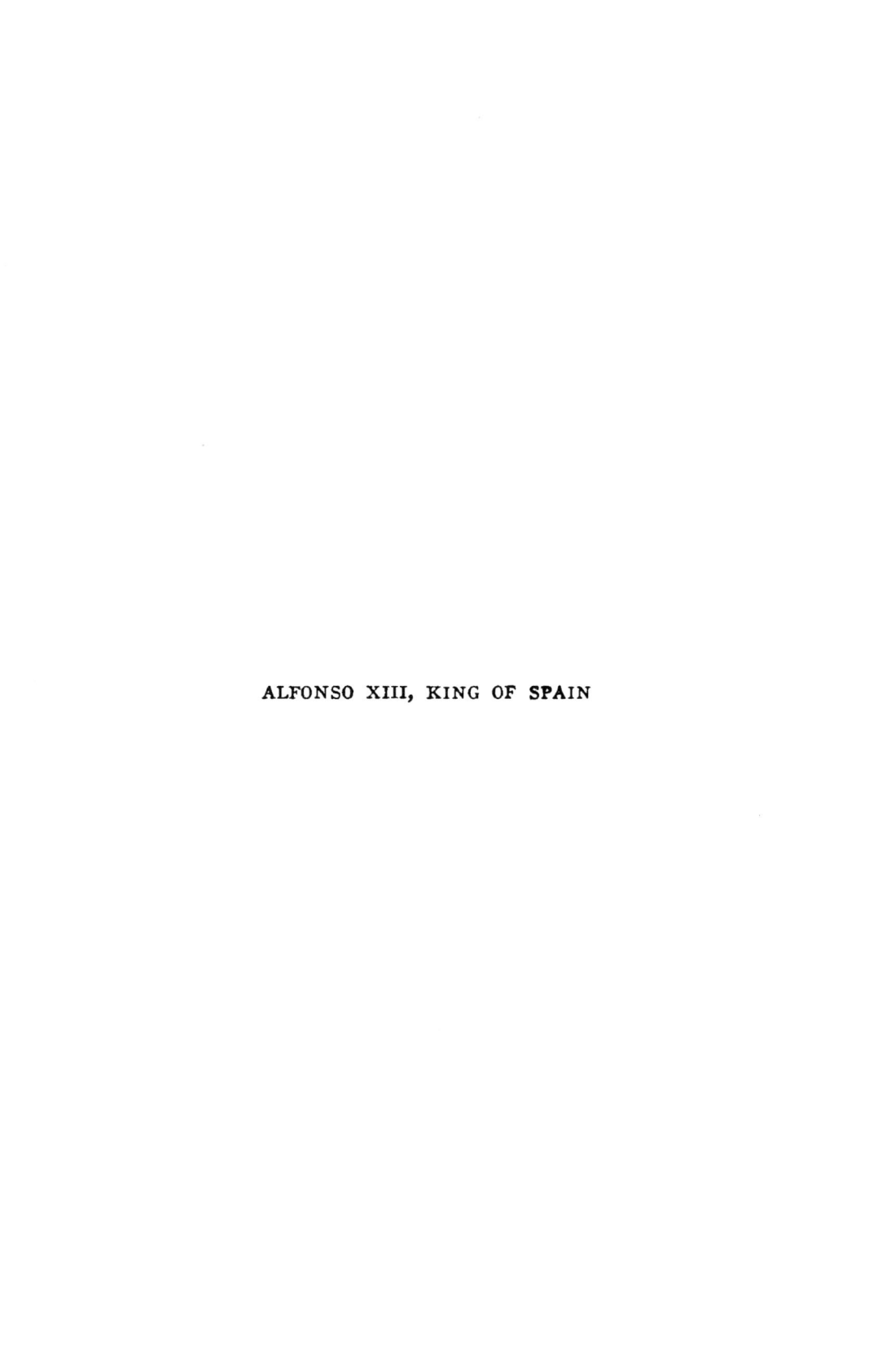

ALFONSO XIII, KING OF SPAIN

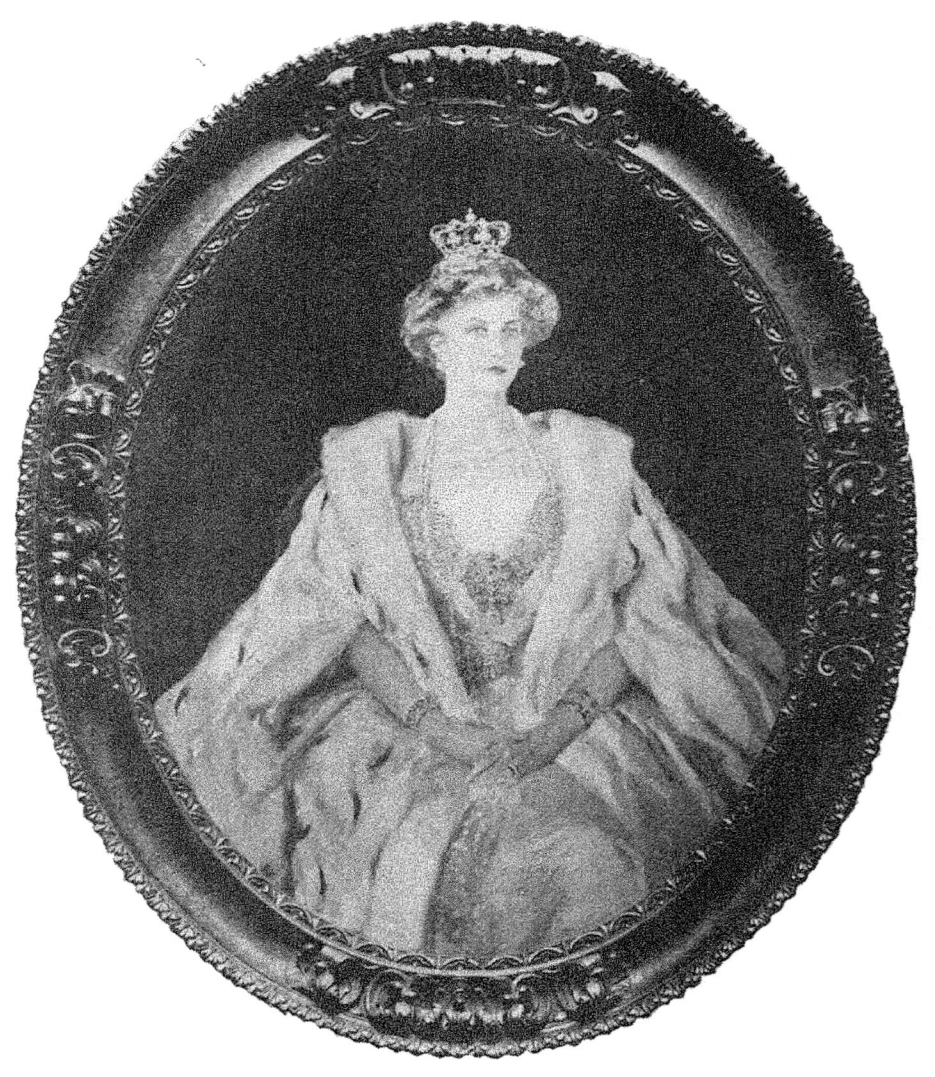

III

VICTORIA EUGENIA CRISTINA, QUEEN OF SPAIN

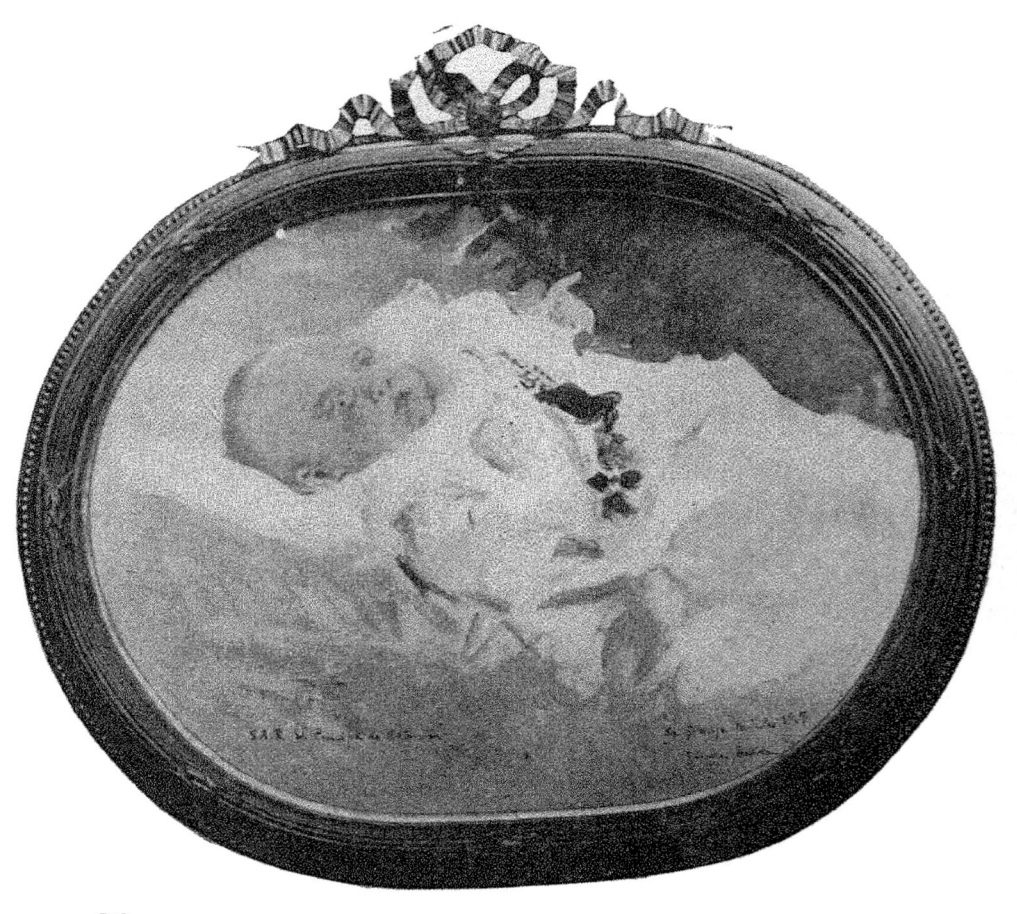

IV

HIGHNESS THE PRINCE OF ASTURIAS

1 Siete-Picos, Guadarrama
Seven-Peaks, Guadarrama Mts.
The mountain so-called, in the province of Madrid, is about 7160 ft. high.

2 Covachuelas, Toledo
Covachuelas, Toledo
Covachuelas, "Little Caves," is the most northern suburb of Toledo.

3 Las Pedrizas, Pardo
Las Pedrizas, Pardo
Pedriza, "Stony Tract," "Stone Fence." El Pardo, a little town of 1800 inhabitants, 40 minutes by tramway north from Madrid, in a royal park 36 miles in circumference.

4 Señor Gomar
A distinguished landscape-painter

5 El Torneo, Pardo
El Torneo, Pardo
Torneo, "jousting-place"

6 Una calle de Toledo
A Toledo street

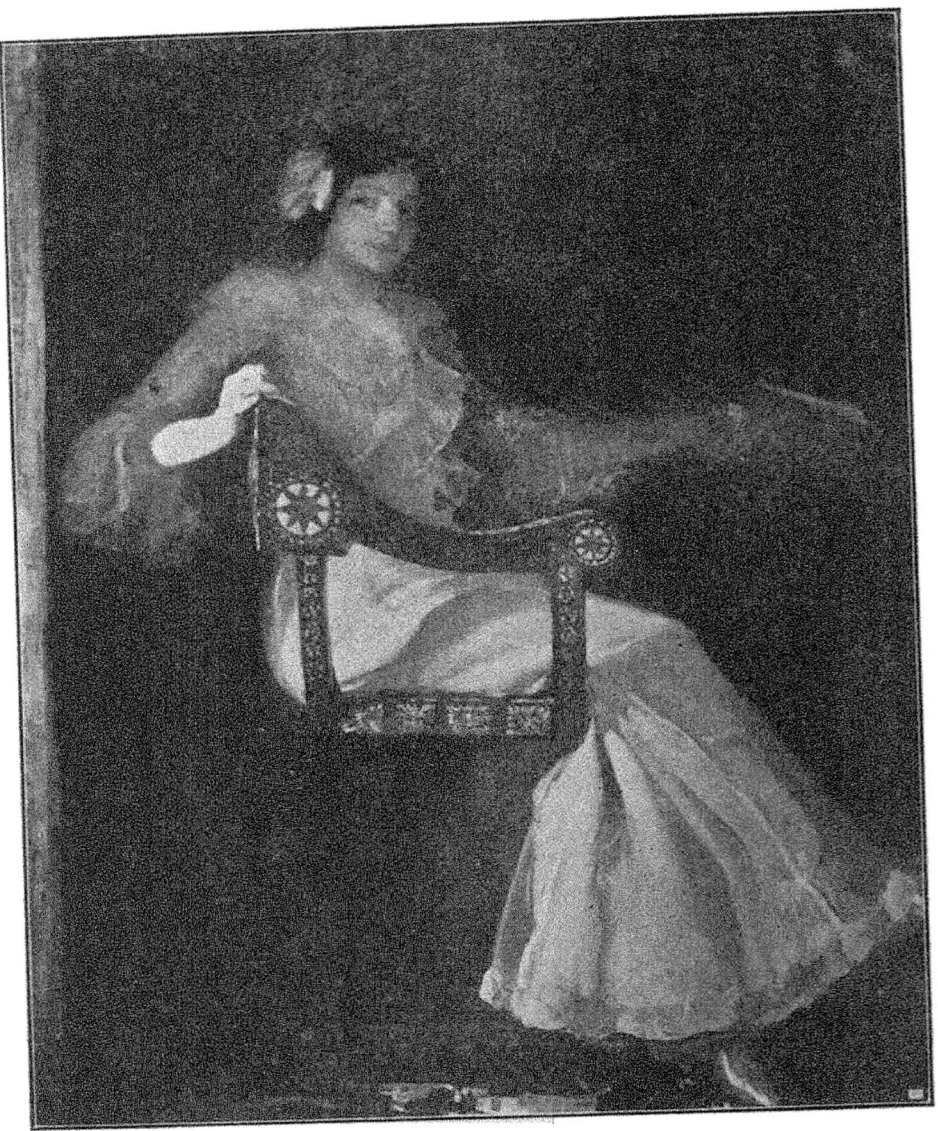

85

7 Vista del Torneo
View from El Torneo

8 Murallas de Segovia
Walls of Segovia
"Segovia is an unmatched picture of the Middle
Ages. You read its history on the old city-walls
with their eighty-three towers."—*A. Gallenga.*

9 Convento del Parral, Segovia
Convent of El Parral, Segovia
Parral, "Vine-Arbor." The now suppressed monas-
tery is across the Eresma, to the north of Segovia.

10 Alrededores de Segovia
Environs of Segovia

11 Reflejos del Cabo, Jávea
Reflections from the Cape, Jávea
Jávea, a town of 6700 inhabitants, on the Jalón, 45
miles south of Valencia. The cape is Cabo de San
Antonio.

12 El Clamores, Segovia
The Clamores, Segovia
Segovia is perched on a rocky hill, about 330 ft.
high, between two small streams, the Eresma
north, and the Clamores, south, which join to the
west below the Alcázar.

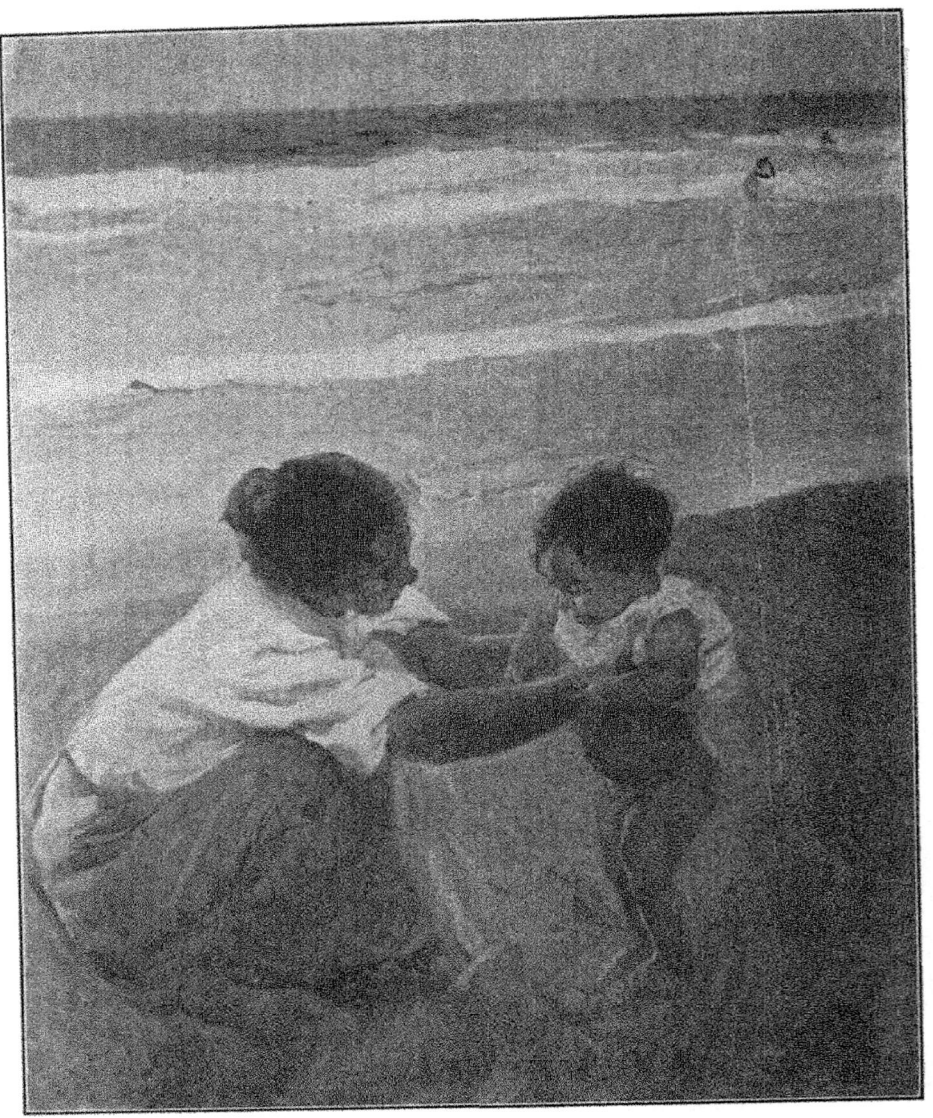

86

13 Rocas del Cabo, Jávea
   Rocks of the Cape, Jávea

14 Alquería, Alcira
   Farm-house, Alcira
   Alcira is a town of 20,500 inhabitants, 23 miles
   south of Valencia. It has many palms and orange-
   trees.

15 Maria en Biarritz
   Maria at Biarritz
   Señorita Doña Maria Sorolla

16 Sombra del Puente Alcántara, Toledo
   Shadow of the Alcántara Bridge, Toledo
   This bridge at the northeast angle of the city has
   one large and one smaller arch. It is of Moorish
   origin (Arab. al kantara=bridge).

17 Castillo de San Servando, Toledo
   On the heights on the left bank of the Tagus are
   the ruins of the Castle of San Servando, erected
   by Alfonso VI (1072-1109) to protect the convent
   of that name and the city, and renewed by Alfonso
   VIII (1158-1214).

18 Dr. Decret
   An eminent physician

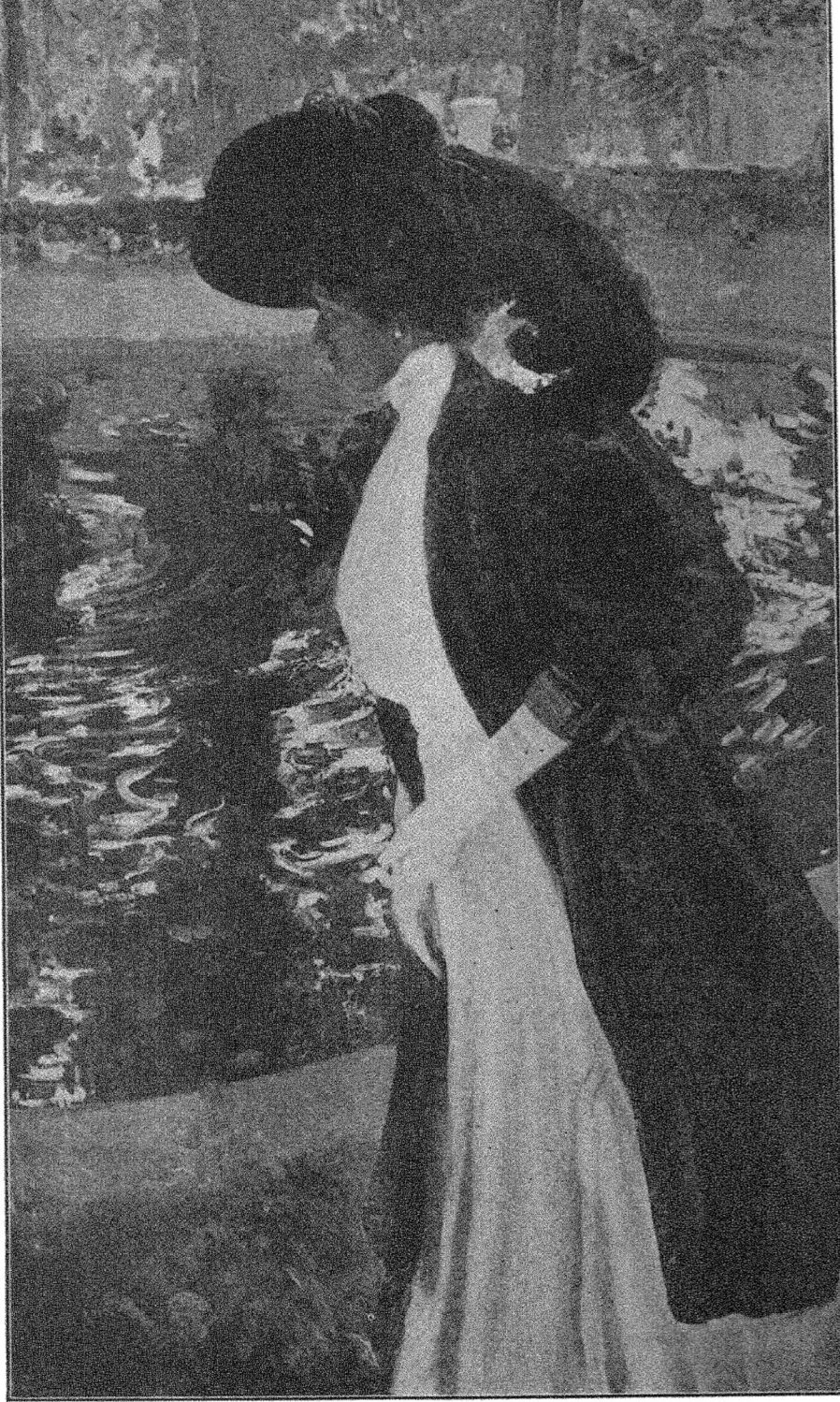

19   Puente de Alcántara, Toledo
     Alcántara Bridge, Toledo

20   La Selva, Granja
     The Forest, La Granja
     In 1719 Philip V purchased the granja, "grange,"
     of the Hieronymite monks, seven miles southeast
     of Segovia and began to construct the château and
     gardens named La Granja.

21   Rio de las Truchas, Granja
     Trout-stream, La Granja

                         •
22   Patio de las Danzas, Alcázar, Sevilla
     Court of the Dances, Alcázar, Seville
     The Alcázar, the palace of the Moorish kings, has
     been the residence of the Spanish sovereigns since
     the capture of the city by St. Ferdinand in 1248.

23   Adelfas
     Rose-bay trees

24   Cañada, Asturias
     Glen, Asturias

25   Pabellón de Carlos V, Sevilla
     Pavilion of Charles V (Charles I of Spain), Seville

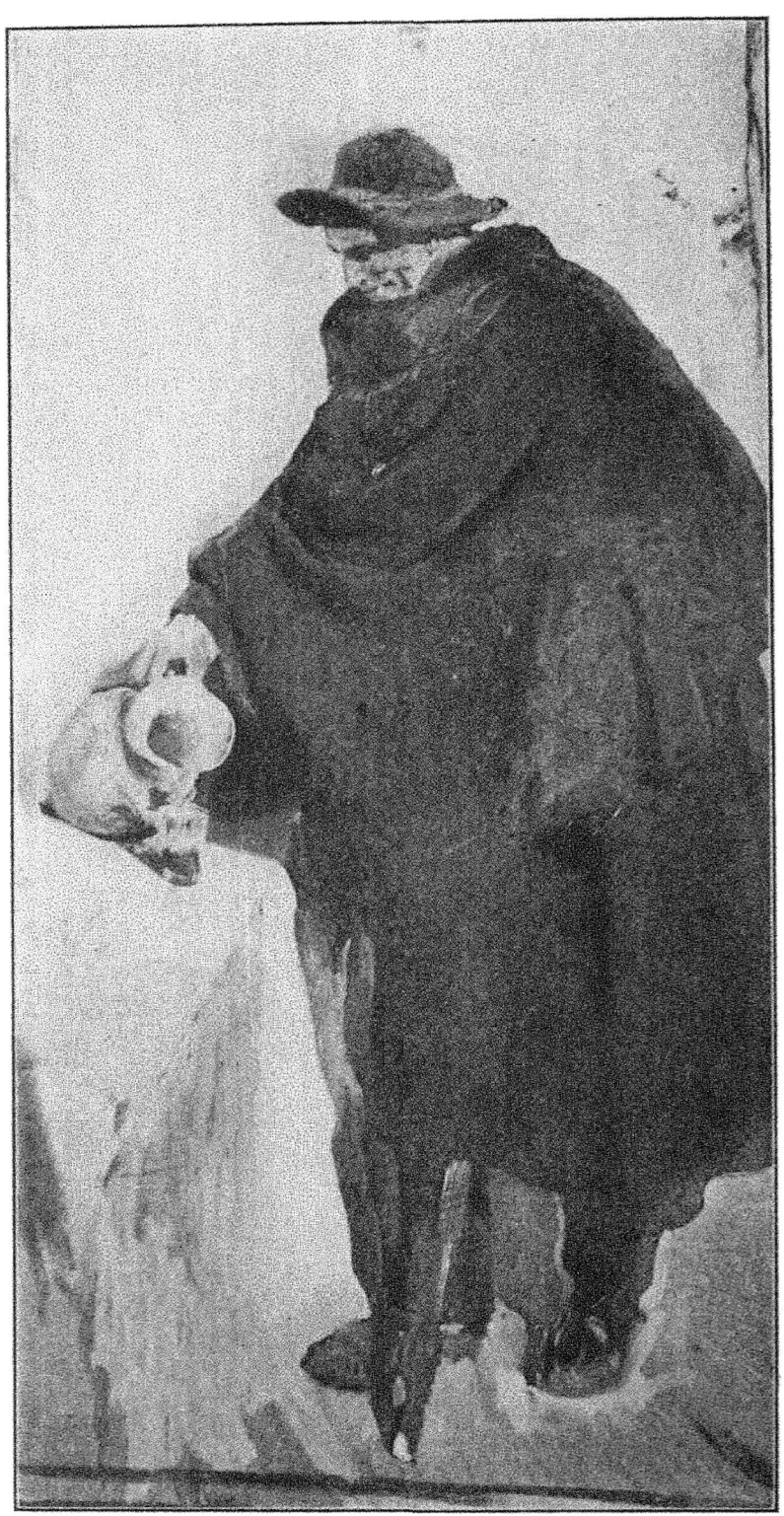

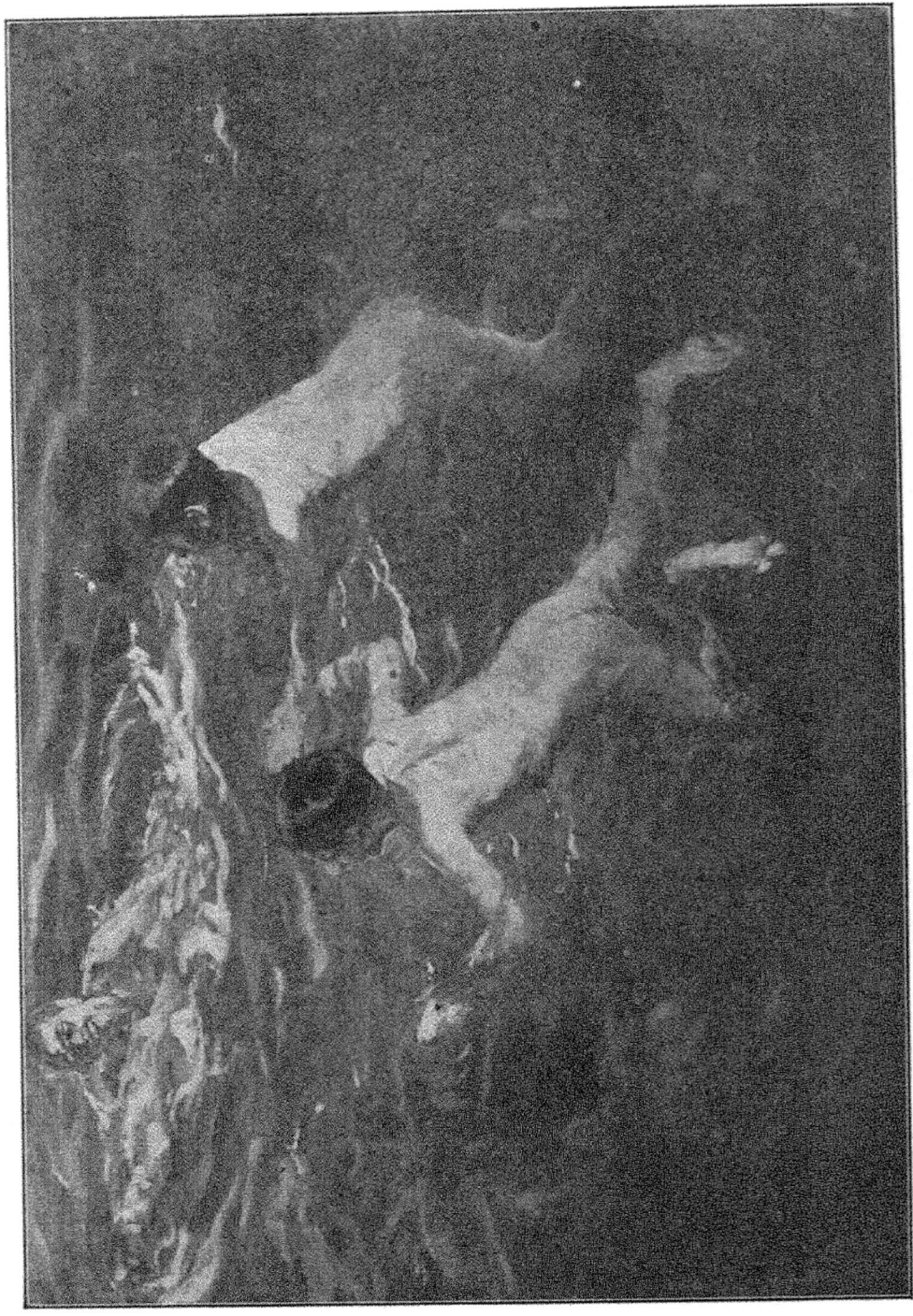

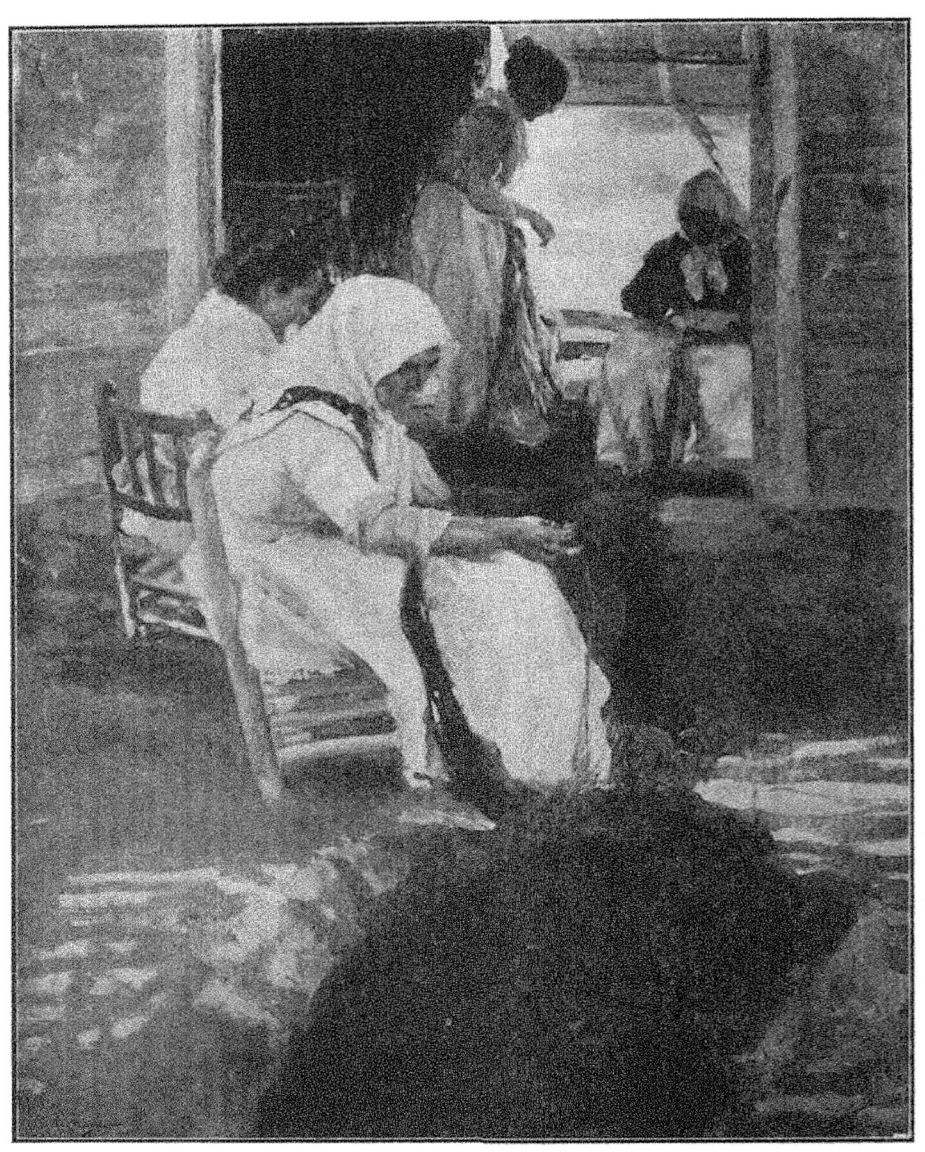

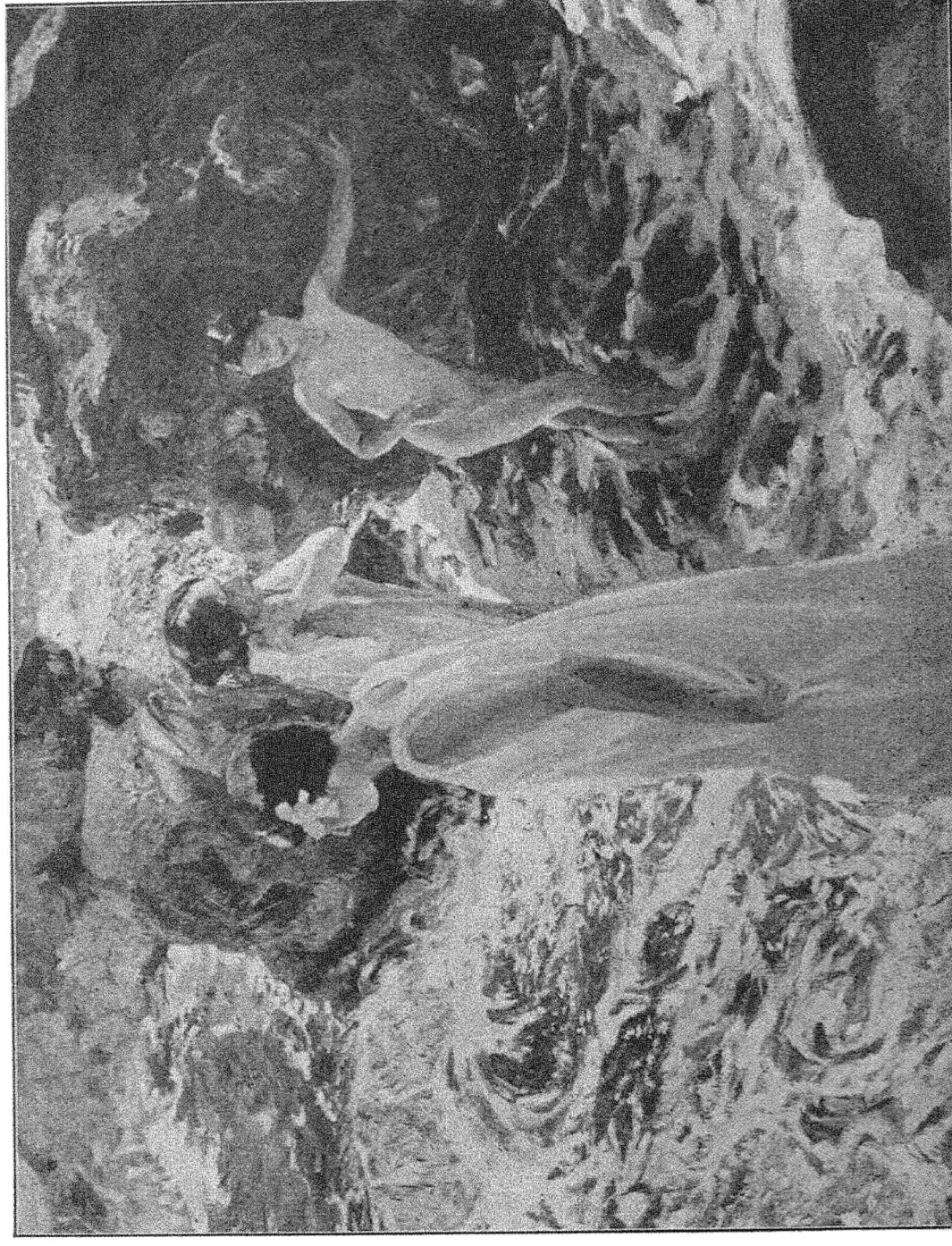

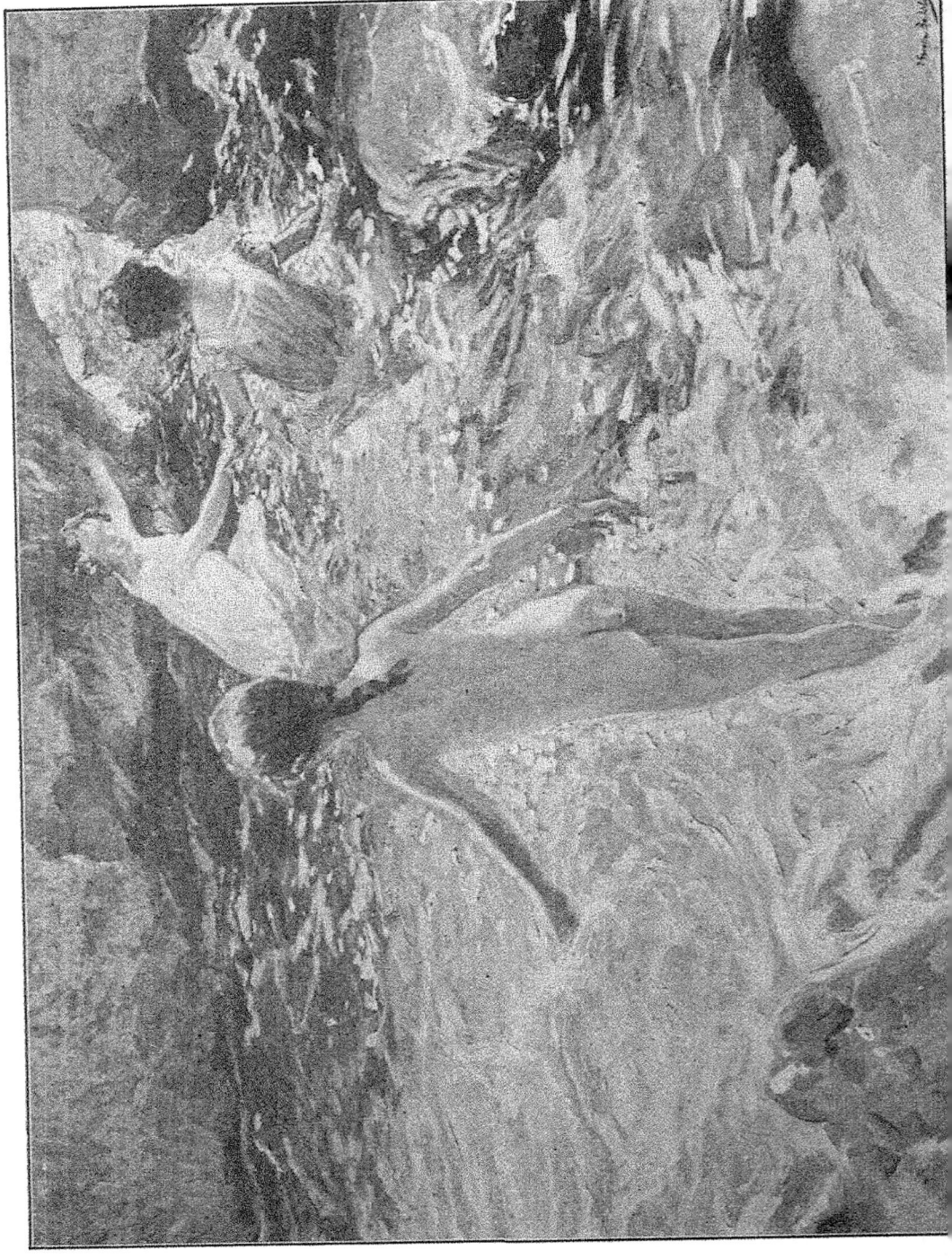

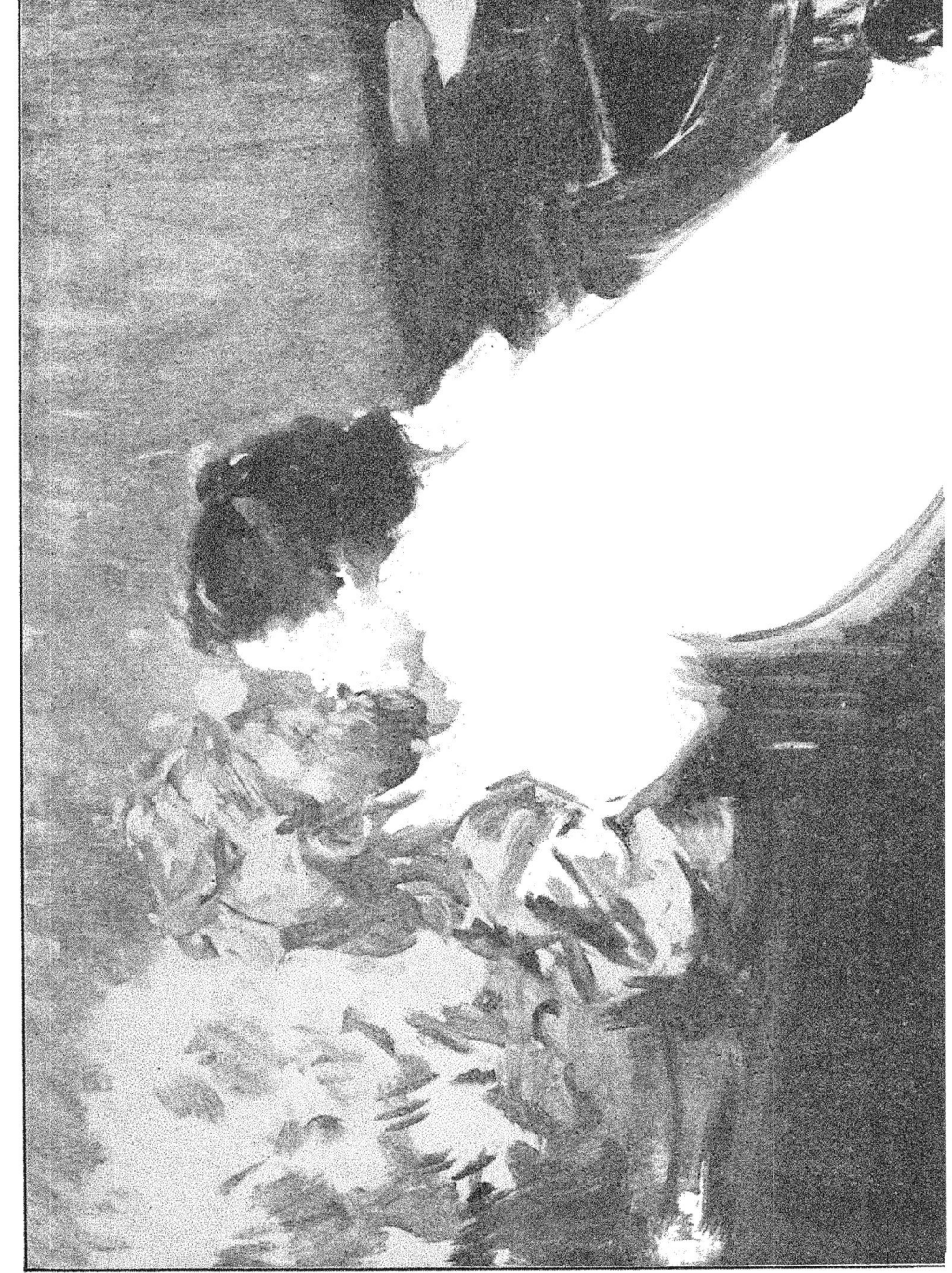

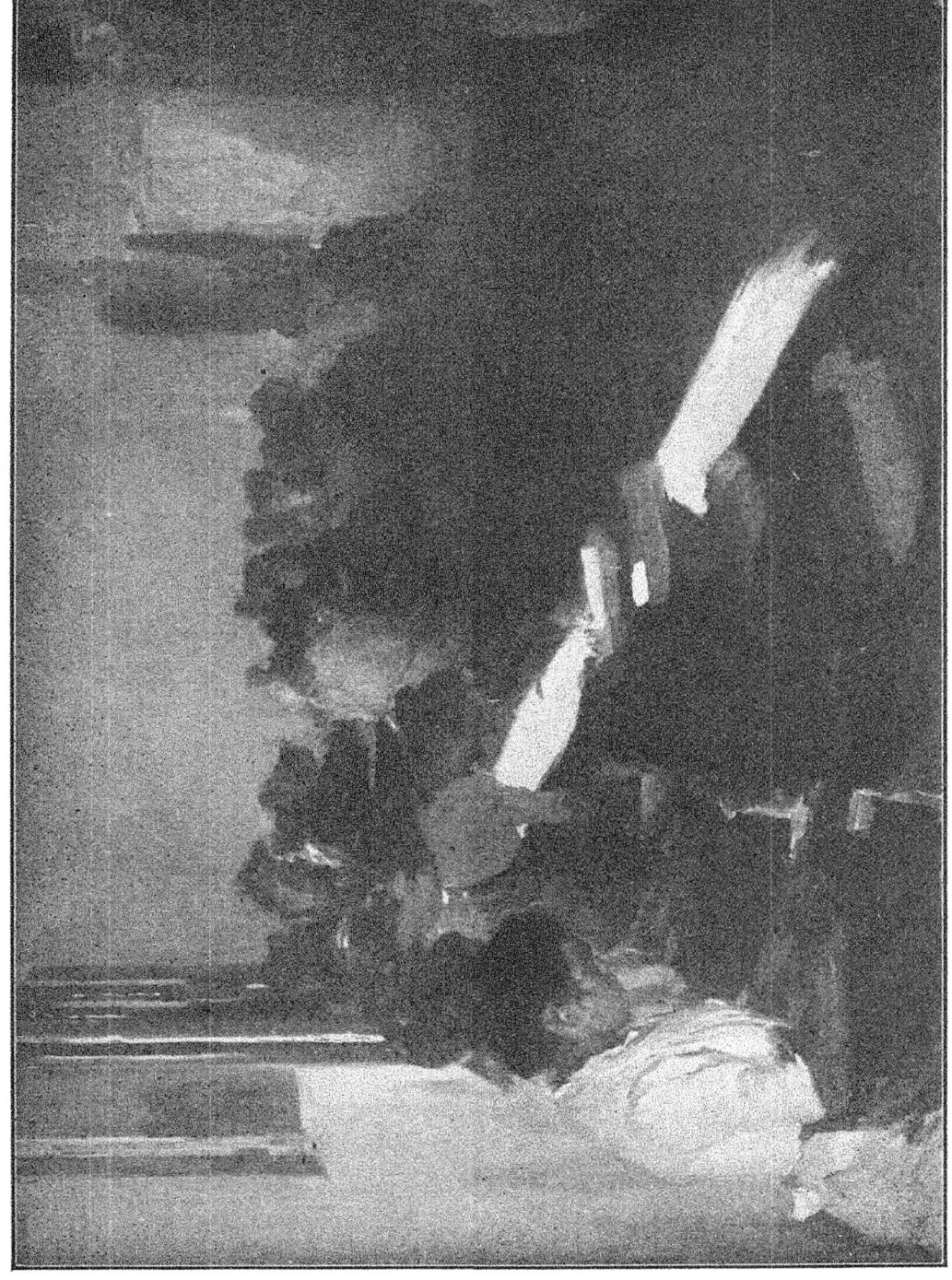

70 Pescadores de quisquillas, Valencia
Crayfishers, Valencia

71 Nadador, Jávea
Swimmer, Jávea

72 Elena entre rosas
Helen among roses

73 Idilio
Idyl

74 Senor D. Vicente Blasco Ibáñez
The eminent novelist

75 Árbol amarillo, Granja
Yellow tree, La Granja

76 El ciego de Toledo
Blind man of Toledo

77 Pescadora con su hijo, Valencia
Fisherwoman with her son, Valencia

78 El baño, Granja
The bath, La Granja

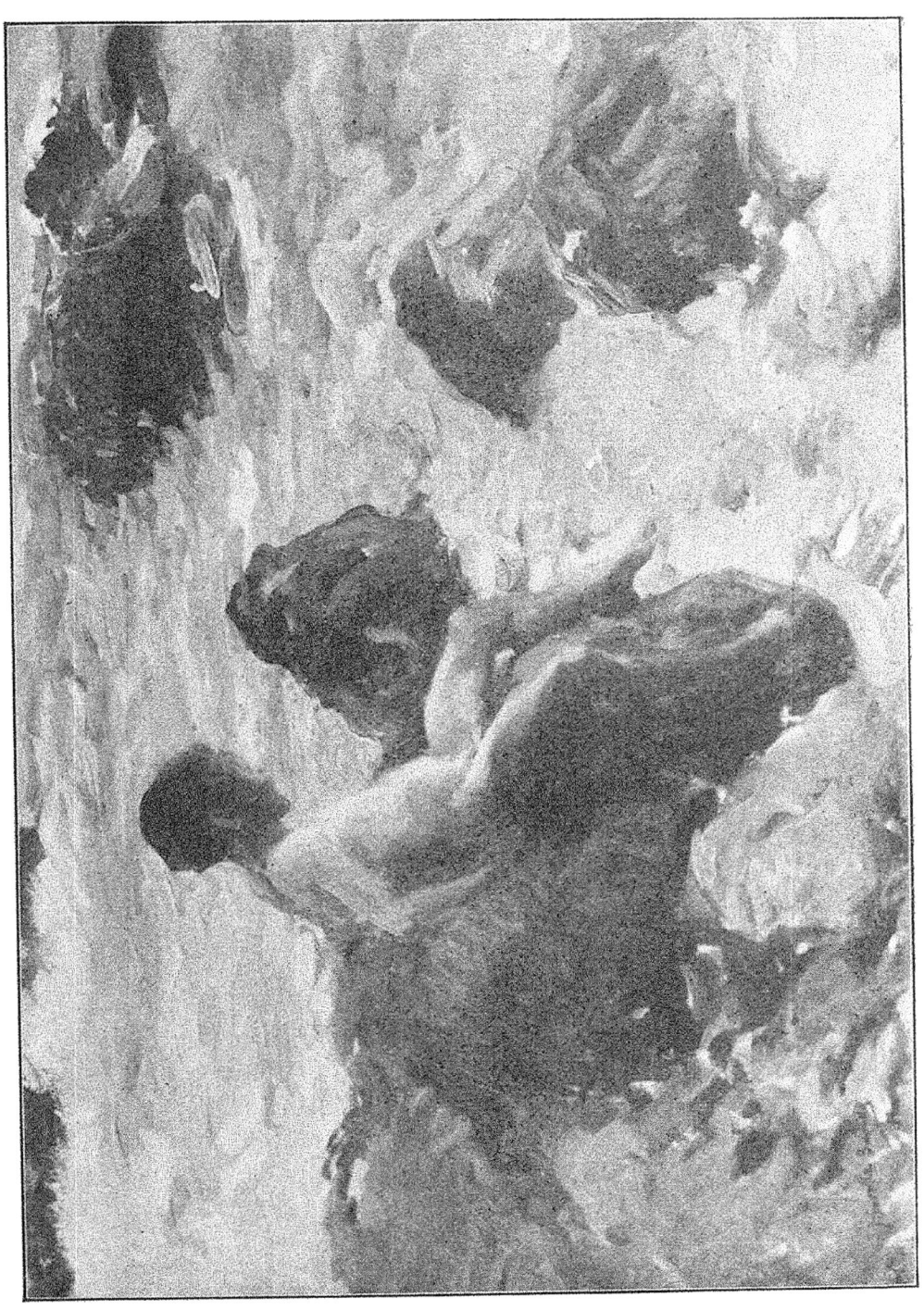

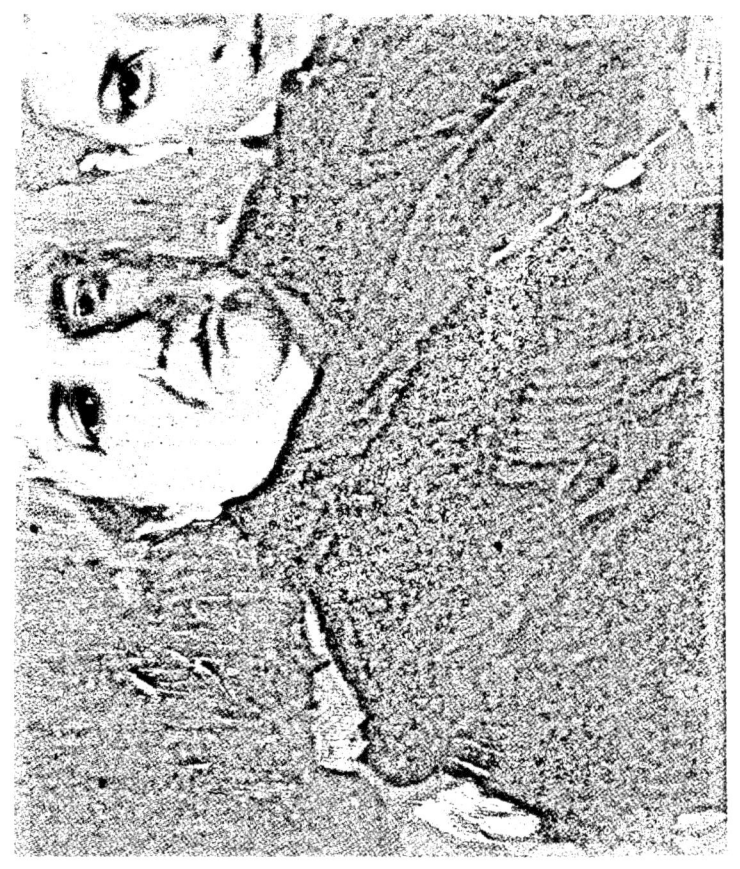

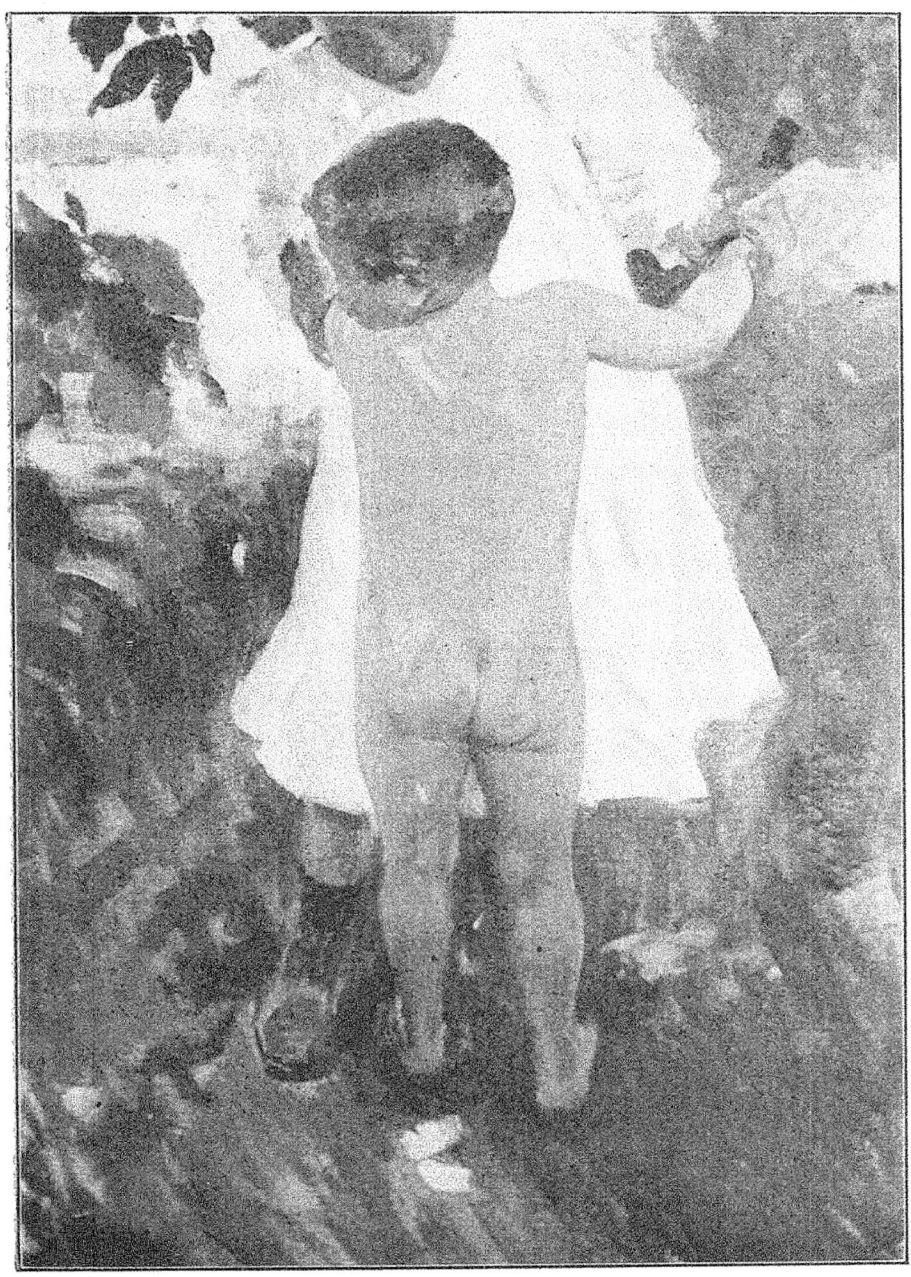

287

288

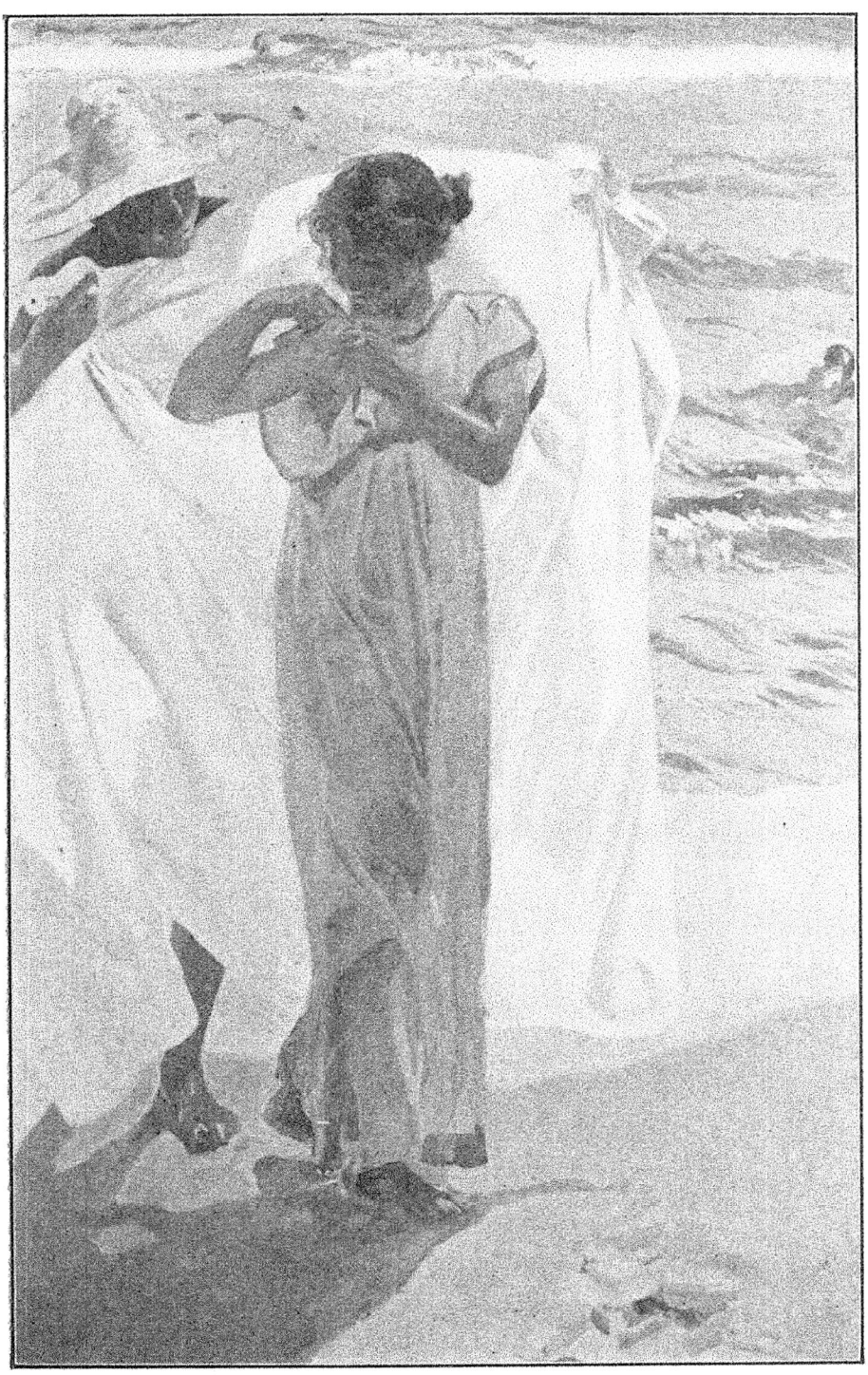

115　La Giralda, Sevilla

This tower, originally the minaret of the principal mosque, was erected 1184–96 by the architect Jâbir. It is 45 ft. sq., has walls 8 ft. thick and was at first 230 ft. high. In 1568 the cathedral chapter commissioned Hernan Ruiz to build the upper section. The Giraldillo or vane is 305 .ft. above the. ground.

116　Palacio de Carlos V, Sevilla

Palace of Charles V, Seville

117　Puerto de Valencia

Harbor of Valencia

118　Marqués de la Vega-Ynclán

119　Puerto de Valencia

Harbor of Valencia

120　Al agua, Valencia

At the water

121　Casa de la Huerta, Valencia

House in the "Huerta," Valencia

122　Jardin de la playa, Valencia

Beach garden, Valencia

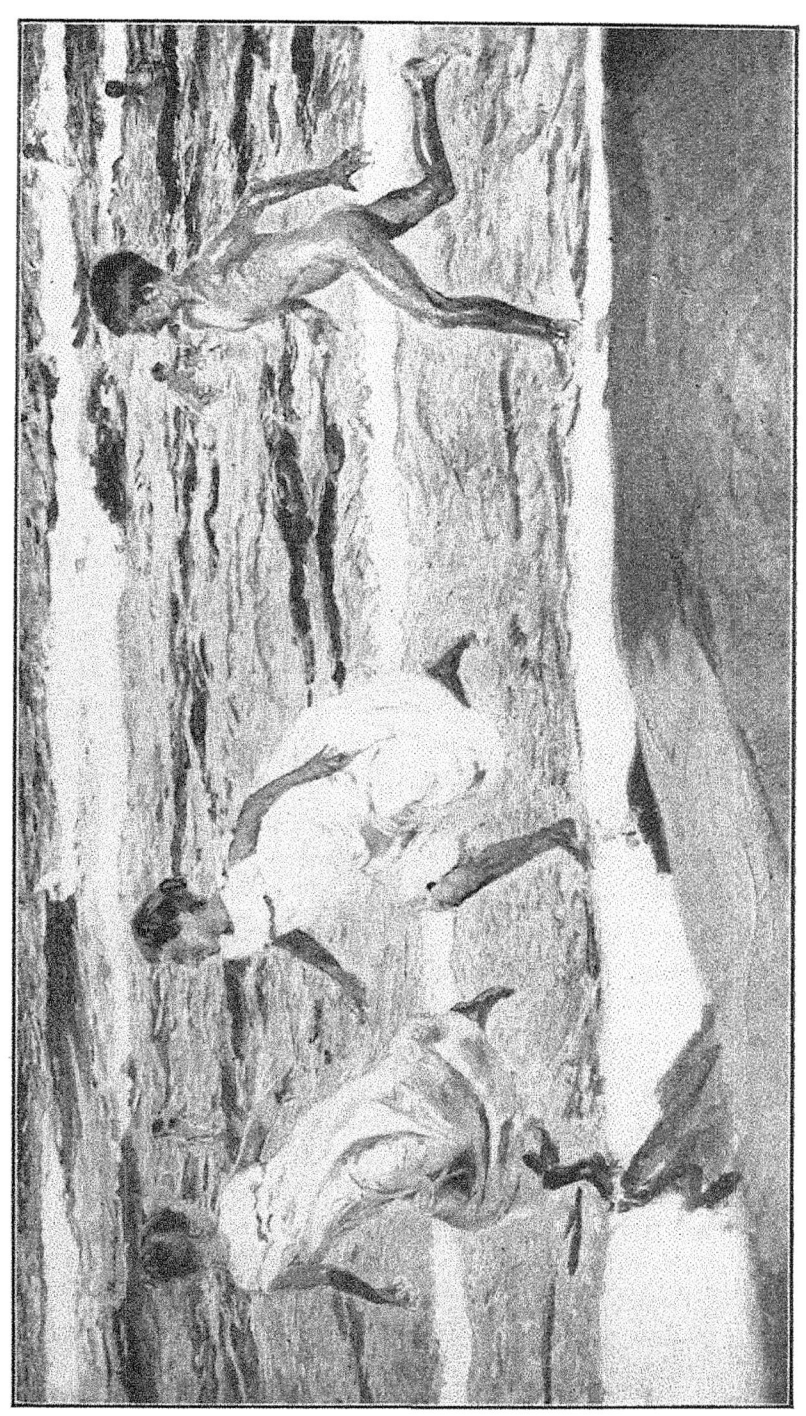

San Sebastián, the summer residence of the royal family, is at the south base of the Monte Orgull, a rocky island now connected with the main land.

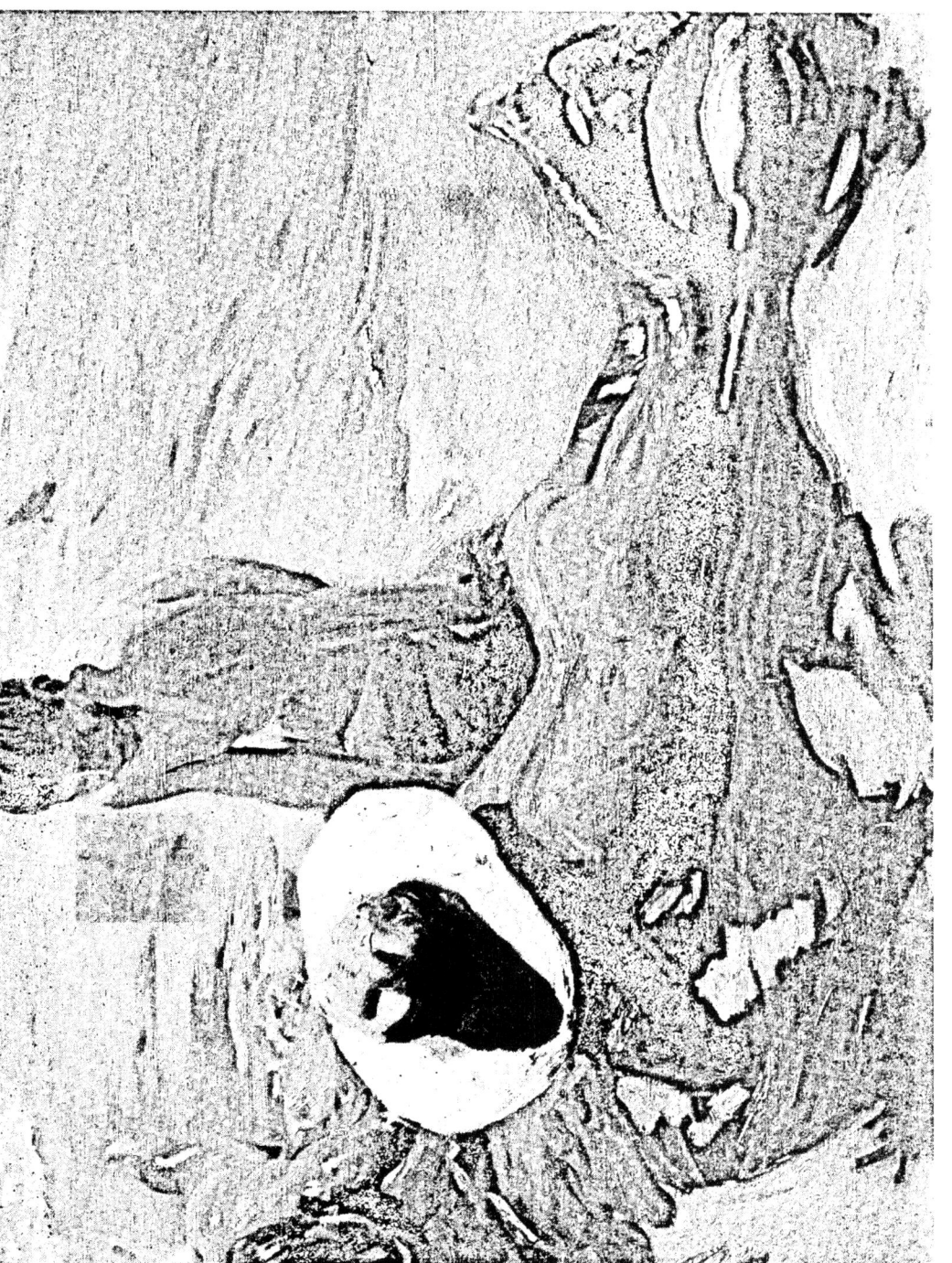

and on alluvial ground between the mouth of the Urumea on the east and the bay of La Concha, "The Shell," on the west.

145   Playa de Biarritz

146   Playa de Biarritz

147   Playa de Biarritz

148   Playa de Biarritz

149   Playa de Biarritz

150   Playa de Biarritz

151   Playa de Biarritz

152   Playa de Biarritz

153   Playa de Biarritz

154   Playa de Biarritz

155   Playa de Valencia

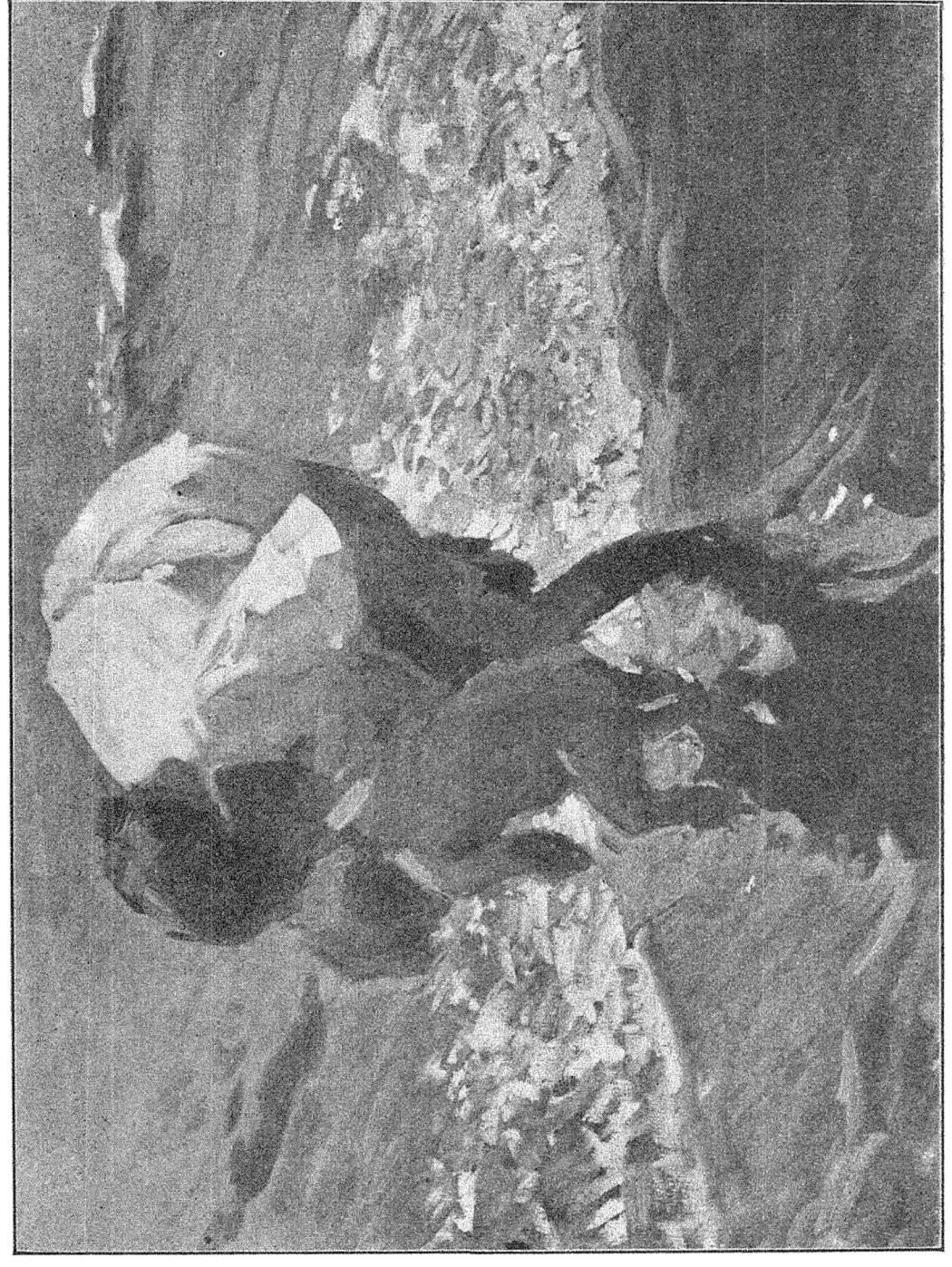

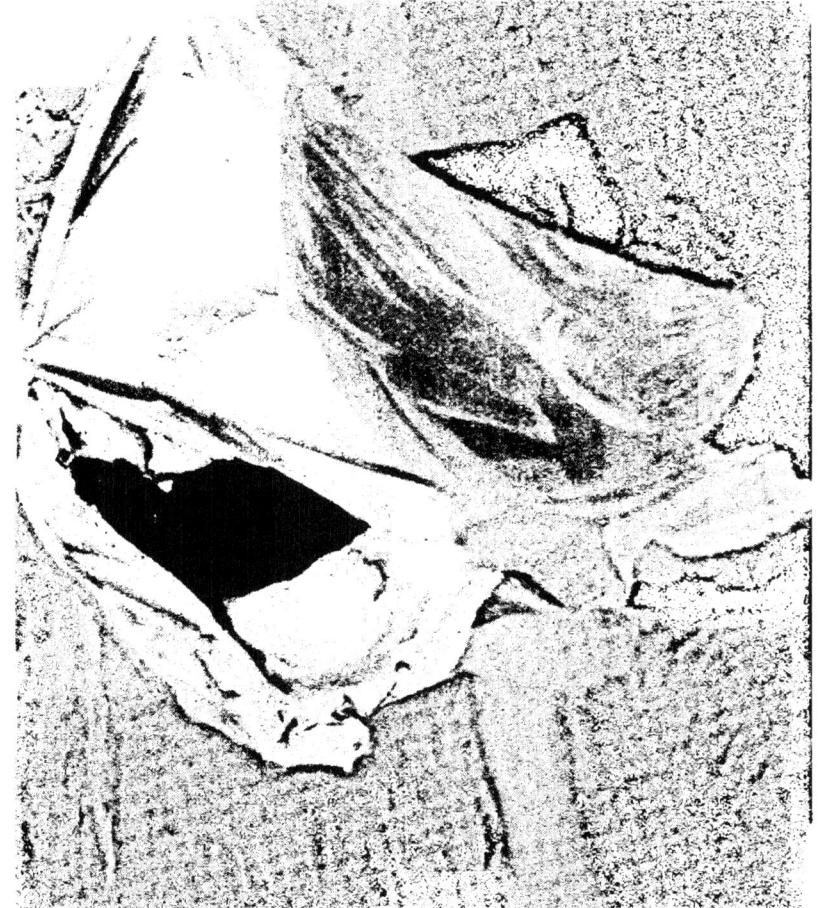

209   Playa de Valencia

210   Puerto de Valencia

211   Playa de Valencia

212   Playa de Valencia

213   Playa de Valencia

214   Malvas reales
        Royal mallows

215   Los geranios
        Geraniums

216   Altar de San Vicente, Valencia
        Altar of St. Vincent Ferrer in the house in which
        he was born, at Valencia, Jan. 23, 1355 or 1357. He
        died in 1419.

217   Playa de Valencia

218   Puerto de Avilés

219   Playa de Valencia

220 Playa de Valencia

221 Playa de Valencia

222 Mercado de León
     Market of León

223 Playa de Valencia

224 Playa de Valencia

225 Playa de Valencia

226 Playa de Valencia

227 Playa de Valencia

228 Huerta de Valencia
     "Huerta" of Valencia

229 Playa de Valencia

230 Playa de Valencia

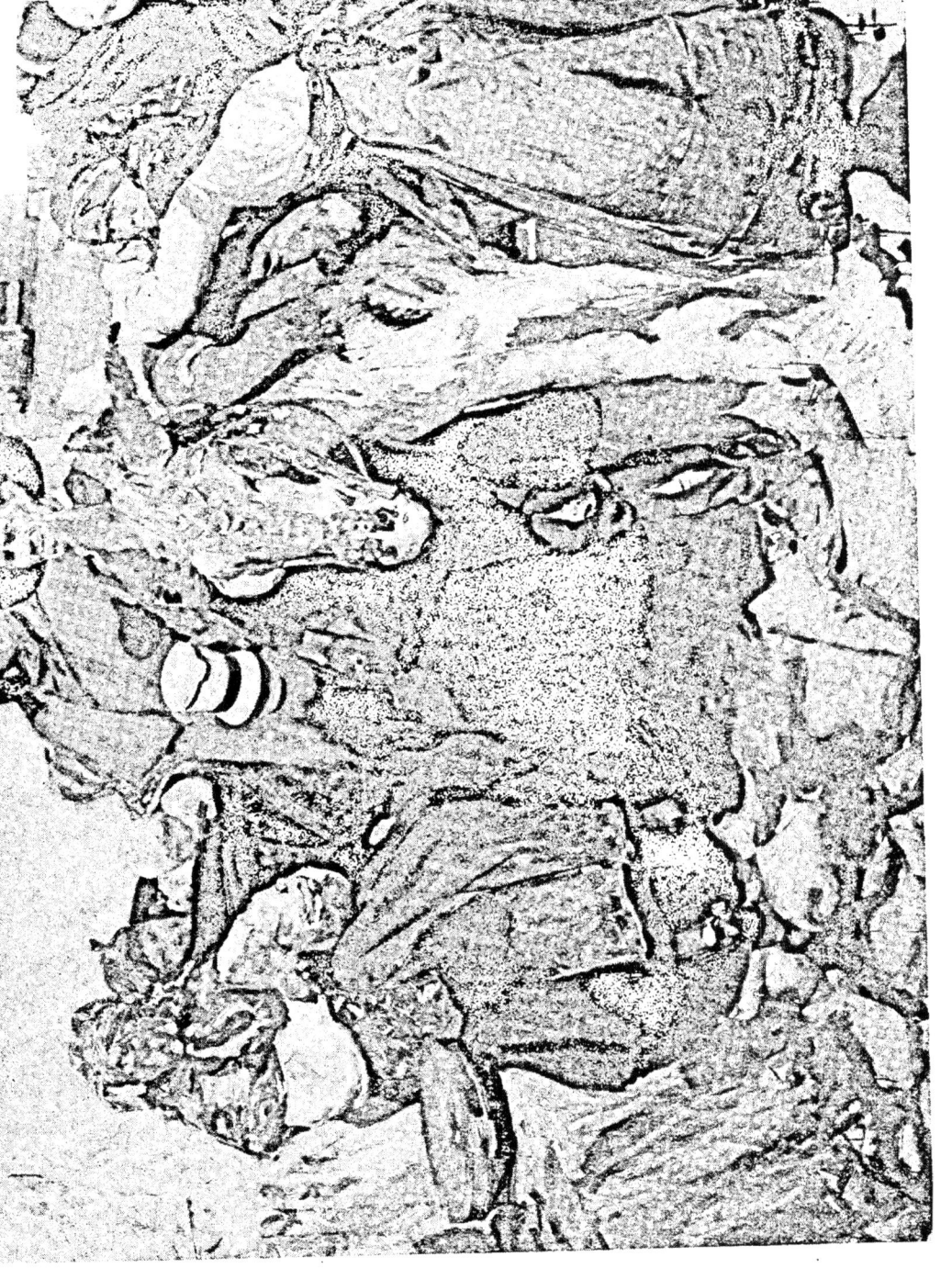

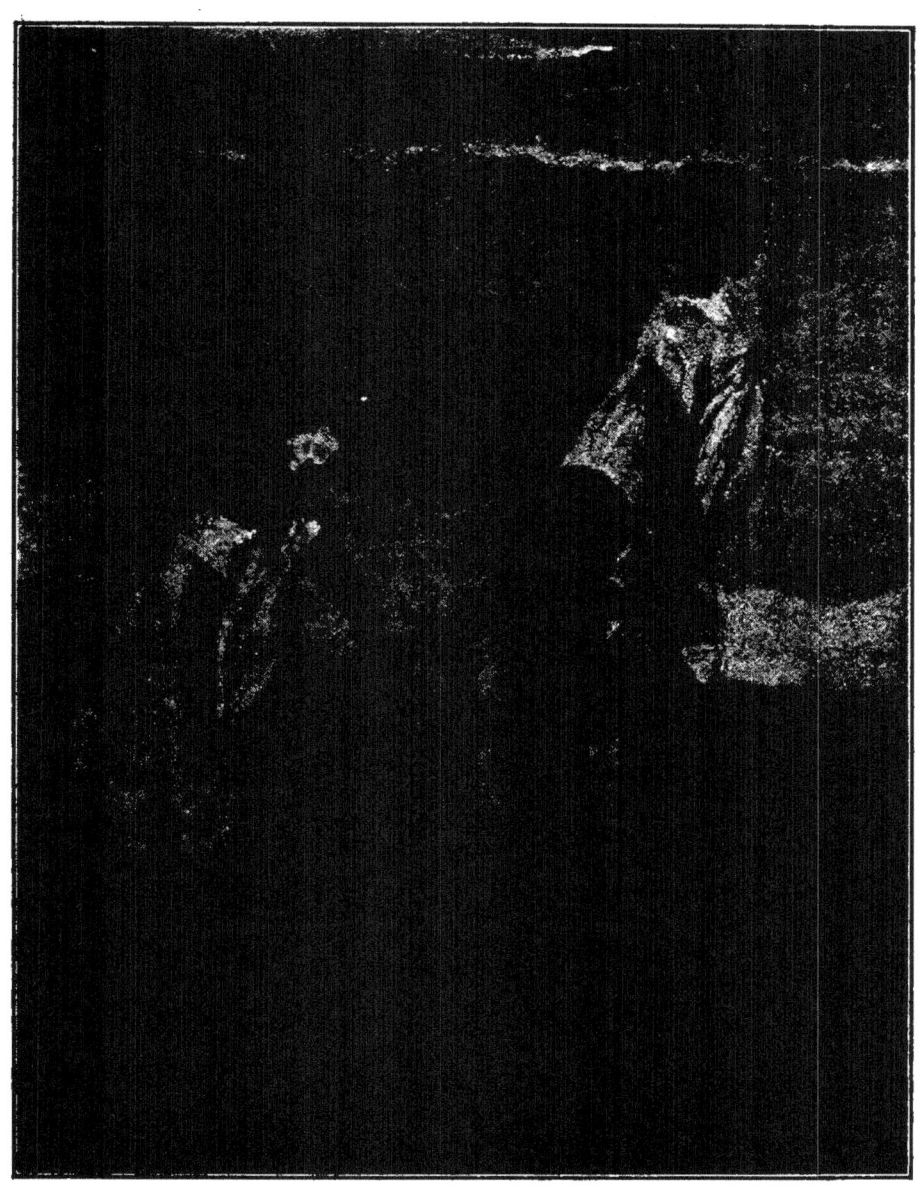

341

266 Malvarrosa
　　　Malvarrosa Beach, Valencia

267 Jávea

268 Biarritz

269 Puerto de Jávea

270 La Concha, San Sebastián

271 San Sebastián

272 San Sebastián

273 Playa de Valencia

274 Playa de Valencia

275 Playa de Valencia

276 Playa de Valencia

277 Playa de Valencia

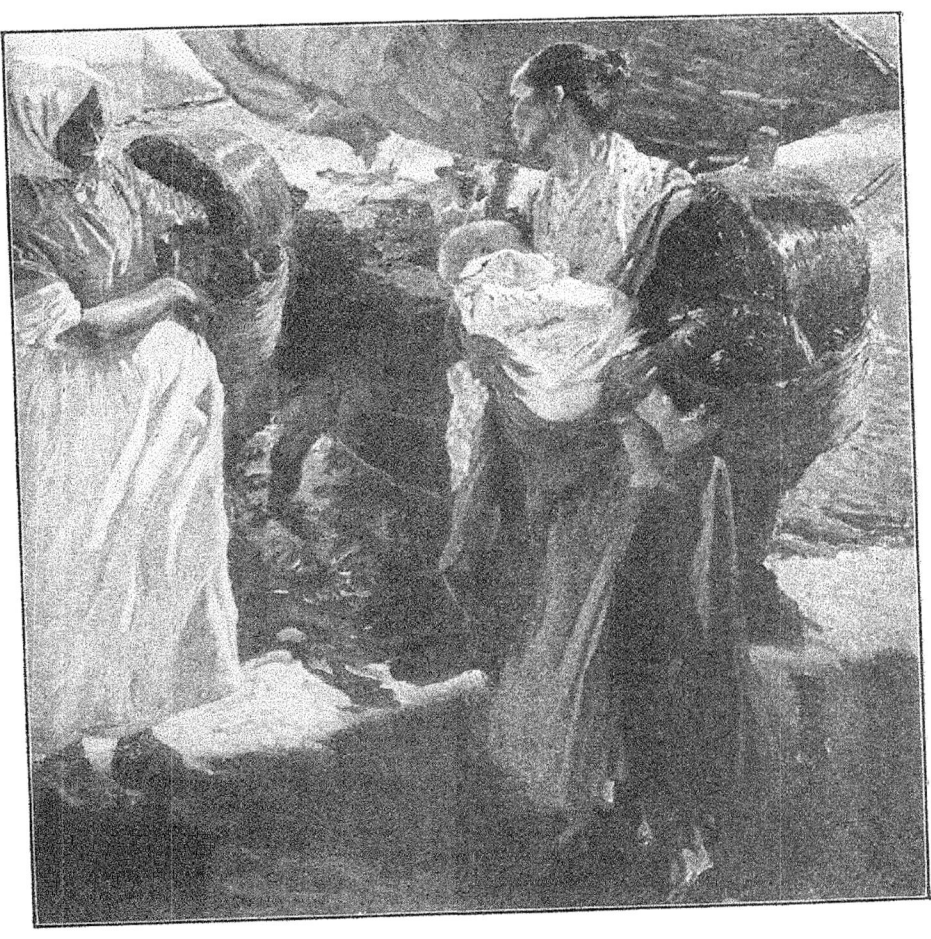

84

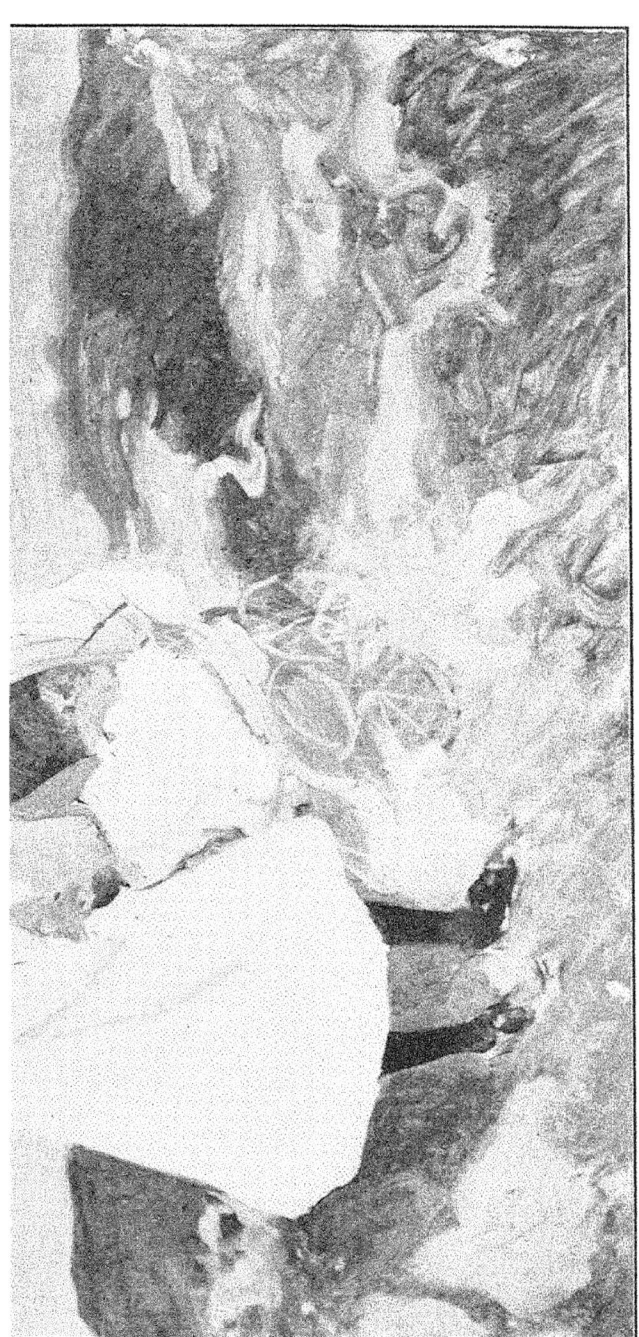

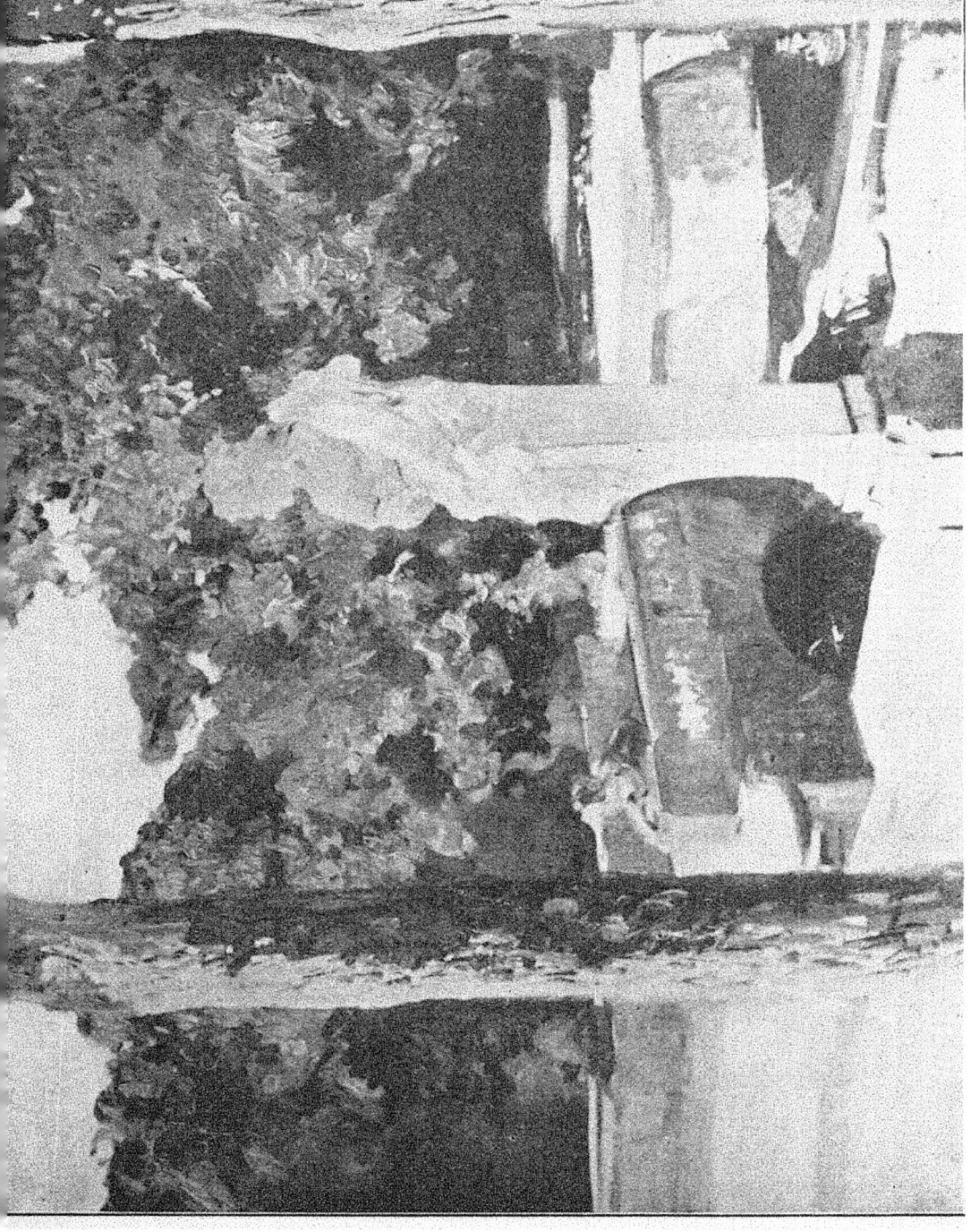

307 **Playa de Valencia (Luz de la manana)**
Beach of Valencia by morning light

308 Salida del baño
Coming out of the bath

309 El nieto
The grandson

310 Alegría del agua
Water joy

311 Sobre la arena
On the sand

312 D. Francisco Acebal
Man of letters

313 Excelentísimo
Señor D. Marcelino Menéndez y Pelayo
The most eminent living scholar of Spain. Born at
Santander, Nov. 3, 1856, at the age of 22 he became
a professor in the University of Madrid, and when
25 was admitted to the Spanish Academy. After
more than twenty years' service he resigned his
professorship to become Director of the National
Library.

314 Excelentísimo
Señor D. Aureliano de Beruete
An eminent historian and critic of art, especially
distinguished for his work on Velázquez.

Printed in Great Britain
by Amazon